Banff Springs

THE STORY OF A HOTEL

Fourth Edition

BART ROBINSON

Summerthought

Banff, Alberta

Banff Springs: The Story of a Hotel

Published by

Summerthought Publishing
PO Box 2309
Banff, AB T1L 1C1
Canada
www.summerthought.com

Printing History
1st Edition – 1973
4th edition – 2007

Library and Archives Canada Cataloguing in Publication

Robinson, Bart, 1946-
Banff Springs: The Story of a Hotel / Bart Robinson. – 4th ed.

Includes bibliographical references and index.

ISBN 10: 0-9782375-1-X
ISBN 13: 978-0-9782375-1-6

1. Banff Springs Hotel--History. 2. Banff Springs Hotel. I. Title.

TX941.B35R6 2007 647.94097123'32 C2007-900733-3

Design and production: Linda Petras
Printed in Canada by Friesens

Table of Contents

About the Author

Aside from writing *Banff Springs: The Story of the Hotel* and several other books on the human and natural history of the Canadian Rockies, Bart Robinson has enjoyed a long career as a journalist, editor, and conservationist. He was an editor with *Equinox* magazine from 1982 to 1994, and the Executive Director of the Yellowstone to Yukon Conservation Initiative from 1996 to 2003. He currently lives in Canmore, Alberta, where he works with the Biosphere Institute of the Bow Valley and The Natural Step Canada. Despite the passage of three decades since *Banff Springs* first appeared, the hotel remains one of Mr. Robinson's favourite haunts.

ACKNOWLEDGEMENTS

More than three decades have passed since the first edition of *Banff Springs: The Story of a Hotel* was published. While many of the people who assisted me so generously with that first edition have since passed on, their passion for the hotel has emerged in others who have helped with the updating of the book, mostly recently in 2007. Of that newer generation, the biggest thank you goes to Dave Moberg, who has been employed at the hotel since 1962 and whose knowledge was indispensable. Also at the hotel, Lori Grant, Ellen Barrow, and Kris Vaugeois helped with details and fact checking for their respective departments. Searching out images 30 years after the first printing of this book was a challenge, but was made easier with the help of Ted Hart and archives staff (Whyte Museum of the Canadian Rockies) and Bob Kennell (CPR Archives). I'd also like to thank the Harmon and Engler families for allowing us to continue to use the iconic images of Byron Harmon and Bruno Engler. I also want to particularly thank Andrew Hempstead, a writer himself and now the owner of Summerthought Publishing. It was Andrew's decision to update the book one more time and bring it back to live after a five-year retirement. It is his prose, as well, that graces two new chapters.

INTRODUCTION

"It had no business being there."

When Morley Roberts, an old railroad man, arrived in Banff in the summer of 1925 it had been 42 years since he'd visited the area. Things had changed. Old man Goss, the fellow who ran the snakebite cure still on Whiskey Creek had long since disappeared, perhaps a victim of his own libations. The town was no longer Siding 29, a random assortment of dusty shacks and tents at the foot of Cascade Mountain, but Banff, a bustling little alpine village which most immodestly claimed to be the centre of the greatest mountain playground on the continent, perhaps the world. And, most shocking of all, there was a castle rising majestically above the banks of the Bow River. The town was hard enough to accept, but Morley found a rock palace in the wilderness just a bit too much: "It had no business being there," he said, "for when I was thereabouts so long ago no one could have thought of it."

Morley visited and toured the anomaly—felt its walls, looked through its windows, talked to its inhabitants—and decided the building, like Banff, was a dream, and, like a dream, at once beautiful and absurd. The castle was the Banff Springs Hotel and it was not a

A 1929 CPR brochure depicting the busy hotel lobby.

A tallyho waits at the front of the original Banff Springs Hotel.

dream. But it was beautiful. If it were absurd, well, there was a method in its madness.

Nor is the hotel today any less real than it was when Roberts visited—but many people who experience the hotel for the first time are overcome with the same emotions which Morley felt on his trip in 1925. The first-time visitor's inevitable questions are nearly programmed in their lack of variation: "What's *that?* What's it doing there? Who built it? Who owns it? Why? When? What for? How much?" To answer these questions, one must go back to the years following the confederation of Canada and read the news about a struggling young company called the Canadian Pacific Railway.

Chapter 1

William Van Horne Capitalizes the Scenery

"Since we can't export the scenery, we'll have to import the tourists."

The Canadian Pacific Railway (CPR) was never, by any normal standard, a modest child. Born the wealthy scion of economic necessity and political intrigue, two well-acquainted if not exactly well-respected bedfellows, its mere conception toppled John A. Macdonald's first government in 1873. Five years later, when Macdonald was again in power and the unswaddled babe once more brought forth, it became cause for some of the greatest uproars ever known in an institution noted for great uproars. Words like "liar" and "coward" were bandied freely in the parliamentary chambers. Liberal doomsayers, tongues clacking like Cassandra's, foresaw the day when the young company would become the proprietor of the government of Canada. But the Canadian Railway Bill, guaranteeing the company governmental support of $25 million, 25 million acres of land, a 20-year monopoly of western trade, and freedom from taxes on all holdings in perpetuity, was passed by the Senate and became law February 15, 1881.

If the CPR were not a modest child, there was no reason it should have been, for railway building in Canada, as in Bismarck's Germany, Grant's America, and Cavour's Italy, was synonymous with nation building. The support the CPR received was an accurate reflection of the young country's impatience to get on with the achievement of the Victorian Age in Canada. The fulfillment of the pioneering myth—progress as measured by the replacement of wilderness by civilization. No one could deny a transcontinental railway would help tame the interior.

"...like the Roman road-builders in primitive Europe, the Canadian railway builders in primitive North America knew that they could best profit from the wilderness, and protect their interests as well, by bringing a little civilization to its barbarian heart."

– Abraham Rogatnick, 1968

Politically, the railway was expected to tie up "the rags and ends of Confederation," British Columbia, and the eastern provinces. Economically, it would give the tiring St. Lawrence commercial empire a bit of fresh blood and pry open the vast marketing possibilities of the Canadian interior.

William Van Horne (centre, with hands in pockets) and CPR officials at Stoney Creek in 1894.

The CPR, in fact, promised its country even more. In an 1889 publication, The Nero Highway to the Orient, the company referred to itself as a young giant whose "arms at once reached out across that broad ocean and grasped the teas and silks of China and Japan to exchange for the fabrics of Europe and North America."

To make good its claim, the company faced the necessity of assuring more than a flow of grand words along the new tracks, and it was soon involved in the construction of facilities to feed and support the trains and their cargoes as they moved along the national artery. The dining pavilion was one such support, arising from an obvious need for passengers to retire for relaxation and refreshment from time to time along a rather tedious journey. From this elemental necessity, the grandiose hotels of the CPR arose.

Such resting spots could have been quite simple structures—even shunted railway cars—and still fulfilled their purpose. That they were not, and that they became instead internationally famous hotels, equated with royalty, representing the apex of elegant living, is due to the indefatigable energies of one man, William Cornelius Van Horne. Formerly the general superintendent of the Chicago, Milwaukee, and St. Paul Railroad, Van Horne moved to Canada in 1882 to become general manager of the CPR. Within two years he had become vice-president of the line and had established himself as the "ablest railroad general in the world." Equally at home playing an all-night round of poker with railway workers or examining the latest addition to his world famous collection of Japanese porcelain, Van Horne traveled from one end of Canada to the other, watching over his foundling railway line like a prairie hen watching over her brood.

Credit is given to Van Horne as the man who"capitalized the scenery" of the Canadian west. Tourism, he maintained, was one way of getting people to ride his railway, and he was very aware of the dollar potential in the Canadian Rockies. Always a man to plunge to the heart of things, he summed up his philosophy succinctly: "Since we can't export the scenery," he said, "we'll have to import the tourists." Accordingly, with verve and dispatch, he launched a campaign to entice the crème de la crème of the international set (and anyone else with a bit of money) to the wilds of western Canada.

The earliest known rendering of the original Banff townsite, painted in 1888 by the station agent D. Clark.

One of the cornerstones of the plan, the establishment of a system of luxurious hotels commanding the most scenic views of the Canadian Rockies, was the realization of one of Van Horne's most cherished dreams. An amateur architect, he took great pleasure in sketching, modifying, and remodifying the designs for such structures. His goal was a series of lodgings to offer royal calibre guests all the comforts of home and still afford all the excitement of close wilderness contact. Who could resist? The promotion for the campaign painted a tantalizing, if perhaps somewhat exaggerated, picture:

"May I not tempt you, kind reader, to leave England for a few short weeks and journey with me across that broad land, the beauties and glories of which have so recently been brought to within our reach? There will be no hardships to endure, no difficulties to overcome,

and no dangers or annoyances whatever. You shall see mighty rivers, vast forests, boundless plains, stupendous mountains and wonders innumerable; and you shall see all in comfort, nay, in luxury."

With such luxurious accommodation in mind, the company undertook construction of three mountain hotels in 1886, less than a year after the driving of the last spike at Craigellachie (British Columbia), marking the completion of the transcontinental railway. Mount Stephen House at Field, Fraser Canyon Hotel at North Bend, and Glacier House at Rogers Pass, all in British Columbia, modelled to suggest Swiss chalets, rapidly became popular as alpine resorts. Glacier House in particular, at the heart of North America's "Little Switzerland," did such a booming business the CPR hired several Swiss mountain guides to live and guide climbs in the Rogers Pass area. Although the architect for the first three chalets is not known, it's more than likely Van Horne played an important part in developing their common design: a three-story centre portion with two wings of different heights extending in opposite directions.

Banff Railway Station in 1888, the year the Banff Springs Hotel opened.

But these modest structures were merely appetizers for a man like Van Horne. While the first three hotels were being built, he commissioned designs for another, larger, grander hotel to be constructed on the eastern slope of the Rockies at the confluence of the Spray and Bow Rivers. Van Horne had taken the first decisive step toward the creation of the Banff Springs Hotel.

It has been suggested that Van Horne originally planned to erect the hotel at the foot of Tunnel Mountain, but that Tom Wilson, a local guide to the railway during the survey, told Van Horne that he knew of a better spot and took him to a site above the confluence of the Bow and Spray Rivers. Regardless of the decision-making process, Van Horne chose the latter, around three kilometres (two miles) from the village of Banff, whose amassed urban potential lay in a few shacks, two hotels, three stores and a livery stable. But if the town were a sleepy little collection of rough-hewn buildings in the late 1880s, even then it held the germ that was to transform a few log structures and muddy streets into one of the world's most famous mountain vacation spots.

The combination of a stunning mountain backdrop and mineral hot springs noted for their medicinal value led Van Horne to endorse enthusiastically the proposal that the ten-square mile hot springs reserve (created in 1885 to prevent despoliation of the area) be made a national park in 1887. Indeed, the village received its first social recognition as early as 1885, when it was named in honour of Lord Mount Stephen's native Banffshire, Scotland (Lord Mount Stephen was president of the CPR from 1881 to 1888). Siding 29, the earlier CPR name, might have proved less difficult for future generations of tourists to pronounce, but it wasn't really a suitable name for an international resort.

Enjoying Sulphur Springs Basin, now known as the Cave and Basin.

Cave and Basin National Historic Site

On November 8, 1883, three young railway workers–Franklin McCabe and William and Thomas McCardell–stumbled on hot springs while looking for gold on the lower slopes of Sulphur Mountain. They were quickly lounging in the hot water, a real luxury in the Wild West. The men had not found gold, but something just as precious–a hot mineral spring that in time would attract wealthy customers from around the world. They built a fence around the source, constructed a crude cabin, and began the long process of establishing a claim to the site. But the government beat them to it, settling their claim for a few thousand dollars and acquiring the hot springs as an ongoing source of revenue to support the new railway. Bathhouses were installed in 1887, and bathers paid 10 cents for a swim. The pools were eventually lined with concrete, and additions were built onto the original structures.

Although the pools are now closed for swimming, the Cave and Basin National Historic Site is one of Banff's most popular attractions. Interpretive displays describe the hows and whys of the springs. A narrow tunnel winds into the dimly lit cave, and short walking trails around the complex lead through a unique environment created by hot water from the springs.

Nor was Banff to remain a dusty little mountain village for long. While cows strolled leisurely down the town's main street in the summer of 1886, and the tourist's dollar was little more than a passing stroke of luck, things had happened in the east to mature a financial swan from an ugly duckling. Van Horne, it seems, had hired the architectural high priest of the Boston baronage, a man named Bruce Price, to design the Banff Springs Hotel. Van Horne's attention may have been drawn to Price by the parlour cars he had designed for the Pennsylvania and Boston and Albany Railroad. It's just as likely, though, that Van Horne, an avid architectural neophyte, was familiar with the works of Price's teacher, Henry Hobson Richardson, one of the great names in American Victorian architecture. Price was commissioned by the CPR to design the new Windsor Station in Montreal in 1886, and shortly thereafter was asked to submit plans for the hotel at Banff.

With all the advantages of hindsight, we can see that Price sired two noteworthy and enduring social entities. Daughter Emily Post, the apostle of proper American etiquette, was one; and the other, the "national style" of architecture in Canada, that of the medieval French chateau. One critic of Price's has stated that Emily's "rationalization of anachronistic social behaviour mirrored her father's ability to do the same for architecture." But Price, despite his irregular reputation, is without question one of the important men in the history of Canadian architecture.

At the time of Price's immigration in 1886, Canadian builders were slowly developing the first acceptable nationwide architectural mode, rooted firmly in the British High Victorian Gothic revival. The essence of Victorian architecture lay in the idea that any structure must have both architectural "reality" and "meaning." As Great Britain had settled upon the Gothic style, symbolic of a traditional past, for its favoured form, the assumption was the Dominion of Canada could do no better than adopt the ribbed vaulting, pointed arches, and flying buttresses of the Gothic for its central architectural motif as well. That it did occur is well evidenced by such structures as the Houses of Parliament at Ottawa and University College of Toronto, both structures of the 1850s.

> *"There is a large class of buildings erected by Mr. Price in which the French architecture of the early part of the XVI century has been used with great freedom and intelligence..."*
>
> – Russell Sturgis, 1899

By the 1880s, however, the central concept of architectural symbolism was beginning to be modified by two somewhat divergent trends that would have great bearing upon the future of North American architecture. One was "organicism," the idea that a building should be a natural, organic extension of the surrounding environment. The other was the "Beaux-Arts" movement, based on the idea that "reality" in architecture could best be expressed through the precedents of the past made bigger and better with the technologies and materials of the present.

Price, although he won his reputation as a master of the "Beaux-Arts," was very much aware of both of the newer trends, as well as having a fine feeling for "good old fashioned" architectural symbolism. Indeed, in the sixteenth-century chateaux of the Loire he found a style he thought could combine all three: the symbol, the architectural reality, and an architectural mode that which he felt befitted organically the harsh Canadian environment. More than one architectural historian has stated that Price's structures were more archaeologically than organically oriented, that they were built more to convey the idea of luxury at the expense of the environment, but Price, at least, believed his edifices to be concerned with both. The chateaux of the Loire, characterized by flat and crisp wall surfaces, steep roofs, a central tower, and round turrets flanking the doors, he thought were quite appropriate for the northern climate, and most suitable for the mountainous regions. As for improving on the style of the past, Price was pleased to note in an 1899 architectural periodical that he had "had the entire resources of the Canadian Pacific Railway to draw upon, and hence it was possible to build with certain materials in certain ways."

Bruce Price, architect of the first Banff Springs Hotel.

Whether Price's buildings were architecturally organic, or archaeological, or symbolic, they did exhibit the important features of Late Victorian architecture. They were visually clean and attractive, pleasing in line and colour, well adapted to a picturesque site, and without exception capable

Bruce Price's original sketch for the Banff Springs Hotel. The completed hotel differed from the sketch in that it lacked the pyramidal portion of the roof.

of exciting all but the very dullest of imaginations. The style, in fact, proved so exciting, so "very right" for Canada, that it became the focal point of Canadian architecture, and Price, unwittingly, became the father figure of a style that remained vigorous until the 1940s. Indeed, so influential was the chateau style that throughout the early 1900s it was the only architectural mode acceptable for government structures. Price's own Canadian works include Windsor Station (Montreal), Place Viger Hotel and Station (Montreal), and Chateau Frontenac (Quebec City), and, of course, the first Banff Springs Hotel.

> *"Whatever is picturesque in a design should be accomplished by the exigencies of the site rather than deliberately made.... A truly picturesque effect can never be produced deliberately.... It can only be had by adding part to part and without deliberate design or intent."*
>
> – Bruce Price, 1899

Although there is little information concerning the cost or actual construction of the first Banff Springs, it would appear that work on the foundations commenced as early as the fall of 1886, the same year the plans were commissioned. The labour for the job was undoubtedly supplied by a crew of railway workers. Many of them were Chinese, brought to Banff specifically to work on the hotel, as the local labour force at that time would not have exceeded sixty to seventy men.

Despite the shortage of actual construction detail, there does exist, mainly in old newspapers, a certain amount of more general information about the proposed hotel. As any event involving a high degree of imagination and boldness, or great amounts of capital, will engage the public's curiosity, so the idea of the Banff Springs

One of the earliest photos of the Banff Springs Hotel, taken just after its opening in 1888.

Hotel caught the fancy of a certain portion of the Canadian public. People across the nation were interested in news concerning this tribute to elegance under construction in a region that seemed as coarse and unsettled as the image of the country itself. An article in the *Winnipeg Sun*, dated 1887 and entitled "The Great Hotel: A few Facts About the Mammouth [sic] Building as Being Erected at Banff'," gave Manitobans the latest information on the building:

"The hotel, which will be built by the company, the work being done under the supervision of their own officials, is to be a mammouth [sic] affair, and to contain 250 beds. It is to be constructed entirely of timber, three stories in height with a dormer in the roof, and

a basement excavated in rock; it will be in two main wings, the front being the largest, and this will contain a rotunda, rising to the height of the building, and an elevator. The rear wing will be devoted mainly to the commissariat and domestic apartments. The hotel will have its own gas and water works, and also be supplied with electric lights and electric appliances."

An 1888 illustration of the Banff Springs Hotel.

In architectural fact, the building emerged a somewhat different creature from the one for which General Superintendent Whyte carried blueprints across the nation. No one seems to remember the name of, or even admit knowledge of, the CPR official who was in charge of the construction, but it is well known and recorded that when Van Horne cheerily eased his ample girth into Banff in the summer of 1887, he found the rapidly rising hotel turned 180 degrees from what the plans called for. This had the somewhat disastrous effect of affording the kitchen staff the "million-dollar view" of the confluence of the Bow and the Spray, and left the guests in their rotunda viewing the pine trees on the flanks of Sulphur Mountain. Van Horne was not amused. As one of his colleagues stated, "Van Horne was one of the most considerate and even-tempered of men, but when an explosion came it was magnificent." However, even in its most explosive moments, Van Horne's mind continued to function smoothly and deliberately, and by the time the reverberations of his voice had echoed into the further reaches of the Bow Valley, he had sketched a rotunda pavilion and ordered that it be built behind the kitchen, thus resurrecting the coveted view.

Van Horne's architectural acumen and legendary speed of response were illustrated again a bit later when someone asked about plans for a new railway station in Banff. Van Horne reputedly snatched up a piece of brown paper, sketched in a few hurried lines, and handed it back to the inquirer: "Lots of good logs there. Cut them, peel them, and build your station."

In spite of misread blueprints and any of the lesser catastrophes that seem to be an inherent risk in any large construction job, work on the hotel proceeded rapidly, and by the early spring of 1888 the building was nearing completion. The structure, as early accounts and photographs portray it, was a four-story (three main stories and a dormered roof) frame building, resembling in shape the letter "H," the two wings forming the vertical members of the letter. Van Horne's pavilion jutted out toward the river from the front wing. The exterior was veneered to suggest cream-coloured Winnipeg brick, and trimmed with oil-finished cedar shingles from British Columbia. The romantic medieval air of the building was accentuated by steep-hipped roofs with pointed dormers, corner turrets, and large bay windows.

Debates about the stylistic sources of the building raged. One traveller referred to its being "in the Schloss style of the Rhenish provinces," while another believed it to be "something like a wooden combination of the Tudor hall and Swiss chalet." Yet another was correct in assuming the French chateau as the hotel's inspiration, but then went on to surmise that it was built "as a gesture of recognition to the French-Canadian population and in tribute to the French explorers who had blazed the trail for the Canadian Pacific," a thought which, although plausible, probably never entered Price's head.

Banff's First Visitors

The first visitors to Banff did not arrive for the opening of the Banff Springs Hotel, but many thousands of years earlier. When Stanley Thompson designed the Banff Springs Golf Course, he unknowingly incorporated 14 depressions as part of the challenge. They have since been dated at over 2,000 years old and are believed to have been created by the Shuswap, a native tribe from British Columbia, who wintered in the Bow Valley by constructing sod-covered "pit houses" to keep warm.

And if the exterior of the building were exciting, the interior was at least visually piquant. Finished in native pine and fir, the interior was dominated by a huge glass-covered octagonal rotunda that served as the main lobby of the building. The upper floors of the structure opened onto the central hall in balconies in successive galleries, making it possible for the guests to leave their bedrooms "and gape down at the company assembled

The Banff Springs Hotel in winter.

there." A large reading room, various parlours, dining rooms, smoking rooms, offices and a few guest rooms occupied any ground floor not taken by the central rotunda, while most of the area in the upper two stories was devoted to guest accommodation, many of the rooms being en suite.

The basement held, other than the machinery for the electric lights, promise for the gentlemen guests who tired of the mountain scenery and perhaps their wives—a fine bar and billiard room offered a dignified retreat. A separate building housed boilers for steam heat and a large bathhouse, the latter supplied with the mineral waters of the sulphur hot springs which were piped down the mountainside and into the ten separate bathing rooms and the common plunge pool.

Such, then, was the state of the Banff Springs Hotel when it first opened its doors in the spring of 1888.

CHAPTER 2

VISTAS AND VENDETTAS: THE HOTEL IN THE 1890S

"...the dining room is not so good; being reminiscent of an Italian convent being turned into a barrack."

While many of the early guests of the Banff Springs Hotel might have taken issue with Van Horne's proclamation that it was the "Finest Hotel on the North American Continent," few would argue about the atmosphere encountered there. An air of rarefied extravagance permeated the building, percolating up through the exclusive French service in the dining room, spilling over into the plush comforts of the smoking and reading rooms.

Van Horne and Price set out to create a very specific

William Fear and Thomas Wilson outside their Banff Avenue store in 1896.

type of social setting by constructing an edifice adorned with all the accoutrements of a romantic past, and in their task they succeeded splendidly. "Did it matter," asks one historian, speaking of the early CPR chateau hotels in general, "if their size disguised a fundamental formlessness, their exotic detail was meaningless, their treatment of materials and plan monotonous and artificial?" Not at all, so long as the hotels fulfilled their function and their symbol—a pleasant presentation of refined romantic elegance. If the guests couldn't quite put their collective finger on the archaeological origin of the Banff Springs, they could make their conjectures in a very clean and well-lighted place.

The significance of the hotel, however, did not cease with the establishment of a graciously hedonistic aura for the individual guests. With other CPR hotels in Montreal, Quebec City, Vancouver, Lake

Louise, Field, North Bend, and Rogers Pass, it played an important social role for the wealthier members of Canadian society, filling the cultural vacuum that was found on the western side of the Atlantic. In this era, capitalism, *laissez faire*, and the lack of a federal income tax combined to create great personal fortunes both in Canada and the United States, and the young empire-builders were determined to prove themselves worthy of their newfound wealth. For these people, the hotels presented a chance "to pose in the elegant costume of an age of social class, which suggested that those who entered the ballrooms of the place were invited guests of rank, gentlemen and ladies of importance, squires rather than peasants." And for the Europeans of established wealth, the hotels were a demonstration that Canada was not wanting in proper cultural decorum.

> *"The hot springs... combined with the great glaciers and magnificent mountain scenery, are drawing a large number of visitors, the more enthusiastic of whom declare that Banff is the most beautiful spot in the world."*
>
> – Dominion Illustrated, 1888

Whatever its social province, the hotel was an impressive structure, "a stately pile," as one budding journalist put it, and it never failed to draw inspired praise, however contrived, from first time visitors. The quaint but most enlightening Victorian institution, the published travel journal, has fortunately preserved many of these accolades, and a random sampling establishes that the hotel was "comfortable and daring," "one of the finest structures of its kind in Canada," "a most sumptuous affair, as palatial as a Monterey or Saratoga hotel," "a wonder of art and invention in the wilderness," and finally, even to outdo Van Horne's own edict, "the best mountain hotel in the world."

The guests who held such opinions were a varied lot, but all found common denominators in possessing a fair amount of money and in coming to the hotel via the railroad. Staying at the hotel was rarely an end in itself (at least in the earliest years of its existence) but rather was one of several stops on a long and arduous, albeit exciting, transcontinental journey, undertaken as either a vacation or, equally likely, as the shortest and most efficient route to the Orient from Europe. Taking such a trip was a popular if expensive thing to do, and the idea appealed to Europeans with hereditary wealth, to the robber barons and the *nouveau riches* of America, to princes, to politicians, to patrons of the arts, even to the dour financiers of eastern Canada.

Along the way one could be assured of exchanging pleasantries and practising one-upmanships with the "proper" people, and it was to this end the hotel played its full hand. As one early visitor to Banff so ably put it:

"One who stays here for two hours realizes the distinction between the man who lived in the terraced house and the brother in the streets below...for one either stops at 'The Hotel', or he does not. There are several hotels – some on hillsides set in pleasant parks, others on the banks of the Bow River, and some on the main street of town – and then there is the Banff Springs Hotel..."

The idea that the Banff Springs was *The Hotel* began as soon as the guest alighted onto the long wooden boardwalk of the Banff Railway Station and was

Dave White and Bill Peyto at the Banff Railway Station in 1895.

confronted by a long line of carriage drivers and employees of the various hotels in town, each shouting out the name and virtues of his particular establishment. The din of the rival voices might at first give the traveller the impression that Banff was a large and cosmopolitan metropolis with the greatest array of deluxe accommodation on the continent. But it didn't take too long to sort out the confusion and realize that the carriage of the Banff Springs Hotel, by virtue of its size, platform position, and well-groomed team of either four or six horses, was the obvious choice for those who were serious about their pleasures.

A twenty-minute carriage ride carried the guests from the station through the Banff townsite and across the river to the great arcade of the hotel's courtyard, where visitors

Looking down at the original Banff Springs Hotel from Tunnel Mountain.

arriving by day caught their first glimpse of the busy life implicit in a mountain resort:

"In the courtyard are riding-horses and grooms in cowboy costumes, smoothly tailored women about to go for a climb in the mountains, and uniformed servants standing at the entrance eager to be of assistance to arriving or parting guests. It is a picture that one imagines exists only in reality at some medieval castle in Tyrol."

Complementary colours and images followed the guests inside the building, where they found all the latest conveniences, including electric lights, steam heat, and even an elevator for those too infirm or too dignified to climb two flights of stairs. The first visitors paid $3.50 per night. This charge, at twice the expense of the other hotels in town, would provide "a luxuriously furnished room, a private bath, and fare much the same as on an Atlantic liner," everything, in fact, but the wine.

One malcontent found the main dining room "not so good," reminiscent, indeed, "of an Italian convent being turned into a barrack," but there were always those smoothly-tailored women and live chamber music to dispel further thoughts of regimentalization, sacred or martial.

"You sit at dinner in style, and eat your fried chicken a la Maryland to the 'March El Capitan' or a Fantaisie from Der Freischutz, played by the Melrose Trio – three clever young ladies who are great on the piano, the violin, and the seductive 'cello'. You look out on the mountains from any or every window, and are fetched back from a reverie by an American female at your table ordering green tea."

The musicians would also present concerts of serious music each evening after dinner, invariably causing the young to sentimentalize and the old to become retrospective. Other favourite after-dinner pastimes included a session in the bar and billiard room where the affairs of the world—the discovery of gold in the Yukon, Laurier's new Liberal government, and the threat of colonial war in South Africa—might be put in order any number of times; a moonlight stroll down to the Bow Falls; and, for the European guests, chatting with an American couple, a constant source of delight and amazement for the travel journal set. The combination of American innocence and money proved irresistible for many of the British guests. As one visitor summed it up:

"Some of [the Americans] are very plain people, and tell the story of how they became rich with much

'naivete', disowning the idea of their possessing any special faculty (in which the hearer is disposed to agree with them) and confessing also that they don't know what to do with their money now they've got it, which also seems easily understandable."

Another guest relates the experience of watching a group of new arrivals from the States look on in wonderment as the British guests stand for the band's evening rendition of "God Save the Queen."

It would, of course, be wrong to assume that all the early guests were either study Englishmen out to sharpen up their *noblesse oblige* or ingenuous Americans out to reveal their ignorance. One of the early frequenters of the hotel who managed to avoid both vices was none other than Lady Agnes Macdonald, the wife of Canada's first Prime Minister, a highly energetic woman who possessed a rare combination of cultural propriety and a taste for such earthy pleasures as riding on the cowcatcher (metal grille) of locomotives. Her record distance for such a feat seems to have occurred in 1886 when she rode the 'catcher most of the distance from Laggan (Lake Louise) to Vancouver, nearly 1,000 km (600 miles), even though her husband dismissed the whole affair as "rather ridiculous."

Lady Agnes became so enamoured of Banff during an 1886 transcontinental trip that she had a private cottage built for her adjacent to the hotel. She used the cottage during the summers of 1887, '88, and '89 (and thus she would have watched the hotel being built). She combined her love for word games and her hobby of woodcarving by inscribing *If the B m.t. put : it,* above the fireplace (which translates to "If the grate be empty, put coal

The view to the hotel from Surprise Corner.

on it"). The cabin, known as the Earnscliffe Cottage, still stands on the south side of the hotel. Since Lady Macdonald's time the cottage has been used as a residence for hotel managers and hotel staff, a storage room, and a rental shop for snowmobiles.

Lord Mount Stephen's eccentric nephew.

Another early frequenter of the hotel, the nephew of Lord Mount Stephen, was as interesting as Lady Macdonald, if for slightly different reasons. He disliked hotel lobbies as much as Lady Agnes liked locomotives. He took all his meals in his room and used the room's window as entrance and exit for his chambers, preferring never to cross through the rotunda and use the hotel's main doors.

Another early guest of note, a bit more sociable, was a young, good-looking millionaire named Ross Thompson, the embodiment of hope in that western rags-to-riches myth wherein the very amiable but very broke young cowboy invests his last twenty dollars in two uncertain mine claims and comes through with the mother lode. Which is precisely what happened to Thompson in 1895. In the summer of 1896, both his fortune and his reputation established, he checked into the Banff Springs Hotel, more than ready to mix a little business with his pleasure. It seems that Thompson had been to Banff before, during the spring of 1895, bumming a train ride toward the British Columbia interior and his fortune, and he had been arrested and run out of town for vagrancy. Now, a year later, he was back, but this time he travelled first class. It was doubly a pleasure to be back in town when he discovered that a man by the name of Stellarton was registered at the hotel. Stellarton was one of a group of New York financiers who had tried unsuccessfully to separate Thompson from his mines earlier in the year. Stellarton, aspiring to the select social circle of the "New York 400," was eager to meet Thompson and set things straight – and introduce Thompson to his daughter. During his week at the hotel, Thompson made himself pleasantly available to the other guests, struck up friendships with many of the townspeople, innocently courted Stellarton's daughter, and became friendly with Inspector Harper of the Royal Northwest Mounted Police. He was, he said, interested in police work.

On his final night in Banff, Thompson graciously invited the Stellarton family and Inspector Harper to a private dinner party where he wined and dined them most elegantly. Arrangements with the head waiter called for full glasses at all times; and while Thompson talked much and sipped little, his guests talked little and drank much. The end of the evening saw poor Mrs. Stellarton first under the table and then being carried to her room by Thompson and Manager Mathews, with Harper and Mr. Stellarton not far behind, arm-in-arm, vociferously discussing the possibilities of a national police force for the U.S.A., Inspector Harper, of course, heading up the whole show. A bit later, when Harper was finally loaded into the buggy waiting to carry him back to the barracks, the driver, a corporal in the force, was asked to remind Harper to glance over the police record for June 17, 1895, when he awoke the next morning. Within a day the news of the dinner had spread throughout the hotel and the town—the Stellartons decided that perhaps they would spend the rest of their vacation in a spot where the snickers (many of them from behind the cuffs of the "400") weren't quite so pointed, and Inspector Harper, one would assume, wished he might do the same.

Hotels, and particularly hotels associated with mineral baths, occupy an interesting and important position in the history of political and military

"Wild" Bill Peyto

These words from a friend sum up Bill Peyto–one of Banff's earliest characters and one of the Canadian Rockies' greatest guides: ". . . rarely speaking, his forte was doing things, not talking about them." In 1886, at the tender age of 18, Ebenezer William Peyto left England for Canada. After traveling extensively he settled in Banff and was hired as an apprentice guide for legendary outfitter Tom Wilson. Wearing a tilted sombrero, fringed buckskin coat, cartridge belt, hunting knife, and six-shooter, he looked more like a gunslinger than a mountain man.

As his reputation as a competent guide grew, so did the stories. While guiding clients on one occasion, he led them to his cabin. Before entering, Peyto threw stones in the front door until a loud snap was heard. It was a bear trap that he'd set up to catch a certain trapper who'd been stealing his food. One of the guests intrigue. The great spas of Europe, Baden-Baden and the baths at Ems, were the sites of many crucial political meetings from the 16th to 19th century. Banff, of course, is central only to itself and was fortunately separated in both time and space from the great affairs of Europe. Some would even say North America. Therefore, as there were no doubt other intrigues hatched in the hotel, the major business of was simply recreation and pleasure. Thompson to the contrary, it was highly unlikely that the guest of the 1890s or early 1900s would run afoul of an industrious drummer or high-pressure salesman "with a scheme on." The only real business was to stretch

commented that if caught, the trapper would surely have died. "You're damned right he would have," Bill replied. "Then I'd have known for sure it was him."

In 1900, Peyto left Banff to fight in the Boer War and was promoted to corporal for bravery. This title was revoked before it became official after the army officials learned he'd "borrowed" an officer's jacket and several bottles of booze for the celebration. Returning to a hero's welcome in Banff, Peyto established an outfitting business and continued prospecting for copper in the surrounding mountains. Although his outfitting business thrived, the death of his wife left him despondent. He built a house on Banff Avenue; its name, "Ain't it Hell," summed up his view of life.

In his later years, he became a warden in the Healy Creek-Sunshine district, where his exploits during the 1920s added to his already legendary name. After 20 years of service he retired, and in 1943, at the age of 75, he passed away. One of the park's most beautiful lakes is named after him, as are a glacier and a popular Banff watering hole (Wild Bill's—a designation he would have appreciated). His face also adorns the large signs welcoming visitors to Banff.

the body and spirit in the mountain sunshine and listen to the humming of one's own head in a wilderness silence that had yet to be broken by the racket of an "infernal" combustion engine.

It was, in fact, the wilderness environment that provided much of the uniqueness of the hotel, setting it quite apart from its more civilized counterparts further to the east. For while it was possible to listen to Lizst's *Second Rhapsodie* on a new Steinway piano in the evening ("a treat hardly to be expected in the middle of the Rockies"), the daytime hours presented a somewhat different face, a mad swirl of earthy outdoor activity. Packers like Tom Wilson, George Fear and James Brewster dated their businesses to the first years of the hotel; and the era of men like Bill Peyto (who reputedly had eyes so fierce and piercing they'd make a grizzly bear back down a trail) and James Simpson (who was to become the "grand old man of the mountains" in later years) was close at hand. The CPR-imported Swiss guides were never far away, ever-ready to take hotel guests up nearby mountains. All in all, the various mountain men and the exotic paraphernalia of their respective trades marked a colourful and highly stimulating contrast to the world of correct dress, and most of the guests were willing to exchange the formality of eastern dress for a pair of a pair of outdoor boots and an alpenstock (staff for mountain climbing).

Canoeing on the Bow River, strolling down to Bow Falls, taking a pleasure cruise up the Bow on the *Mountain Belle,* or renting horses or a tallyho for a ride out to the Hoodoos or Devil's Lake (Lake Minnewanka) were favourite pastimes. Fishing was an openly competitive event, the guests vying

A stroll to Bow Falls proved a popular excursion for early hotel guests.

with each other for the greatest poundage—a competition which once went so far as to see one party stuff its best effort with rocks, a ploy discovered and decried back at the hotel when some impudent non-competitor dared to observe that the fish's mouth had been sewn shut!

Winter sleigh ride 1896, with Manager Mathews at back.

Yet another sort of sport was offered by the many virgin peaks of the Rockies themselves, and many famous European climbers were enticed to the Banff vicinity and the hotel by the rumour of untrod summits. Finding the number of unclimbed mountains in the Alps rapidly diminishing, men like James Outram and Arnold Mumm were drawn to western Canada by the thought of whole mountain ranges yet to be named, let alone climbed. Edward Whymper, conqueror of the Matterhorn and one of the elite of the Alpine Club, organized his first outing in the Rockies at the Banff Springs Hotel, although with some difficulty for he viewed the local packers as some sort of sub-species. It was only after Manager Mathews took him aside and patiently explained that Canadians, too, believed themselves to be real people that

Whymper humbled himself enough to engage Bill Peyto as a guide and packer for his first trip.

In speaking of entertainments, not to be forgotten are the hot springs, "hot sulphurous water gushing from the earth for the hypochondriacs to drink, and the halt, lame, and withered to bathe in as well." Actually, the springs proved popular with all the guests whether they needed healing or not, although it is true that the major publicity drive was directed toward the waters' curative powers, they being "especially efficacious for the cure of rheumatic, gouty, and allied conditions," as well as for conditions of "the liver, diabetes, Bright's disease and chronic dyspepsia." The water was piped down to the hotel from the Upper Hot Springs, located above the hotel on the side of Sulphur Mountain. Various plumbing problems often resulted in such a reduced flow of water that little if any reached the hotel's pool, and at such embarrassing times the hotel staff would surreptitiously fill the pool with hot water and dump in bags of sulphur, a ploy which worked tolerably well until the water was again arriving from the springs proper.

There was, it appears, no lack of things to do, either at the hotel or in its immediate environs. Although the Banff Springs can't claim any such bear stories as the one boasted by Dr. Brett's Sanitarium Hotel, which centred around Sergeant Casey Oliver's pet bear wandering into the hotel one night and deciding to climb into bed with one of the unsuspecting guests, it could never be said that any early Banff Springs visitor ever died of boredom.

The hotel and its traffic were bound to have an effect on "the man in the streets below," and the little town of Banff was as quick to capitalize the tourist as Van Horne had been to capitalize the scenery. By 1900 the village had managed to transport itself from the foot of Cascade Mountain to the foot of Tunnel Mountain, and small shops, restaurants, and new hotels leapt forth from the wilderness to create a bustling Banff Avenue.

Guides and packers found the area lucrative. Someone, after all, had to provide services for those "halt, lame, and withered," that came to cast aside their crutches at the various hot springs establishments. The Banff Springs, the largest hotel and entertaining the wealthiest clientele, and having the resources of the CPR to back any innovations to bring yet more people to the area, played a rather critical role in the Banff economy. "The Banff Springs," one resident has unromantically reminisced, "was Banff's bread and butter."

The town grew rapidly through the 1890s, and most visitors discovered the townspeople to be a congenial sort, although there are reports the business community was inclined to be a bit overly-concerned with its own importance, something not too alarming since such concern seems to be the nature of business communities everywhere. It's probably true, though, that one of the travel journal set was being a bit callous when he wrote in 1895 that:

"Not that the town of Banff has much to boast of. It has a few hundred inhabitants, who have succeeded in making the surrounding woods and mountains more destitute of bird and beast and flower than a Park at Montreal. Though it consists of but a single

street, it is horribly over civilized. It has even a chemist, from whom, as far back as three or four years ago, you could buy Kipling's books in the unauthorised editions published by the Harpers."

Destitution, over-civilization, and Kipling's books to the contrary, the town seems to have had a good heart—young Ross Thompson, on his first unfortunate journey through Banff, was given a gift of cheese and bread, no questions asked, by an old French grocer. The act, incidentally, was not forgotten by Thompson on his second journey to town – on that occasion he managed to visit "Frenchy" once each day, buying a bit of candy for the grocer's children and paying for it with a five-dollar gold piece.

The town was able to overlook most aspersions cast its way from the "castle on the hill." In later years the hotel's "snob element" would rankle some of the community's aspiring socialites just as surely as the hotel's platform privileges at the railway station would rankle other hotel owners, but there was certainly no such gulf in the first two decades of the hotel's existence. The town managed to maintain a pride in the hotel that bordered on boosterism, and an article in an early issue of the local paper, after describing the beauties of the building, goes so far as to grant it immunity from the world of finance:

"We tried both principal hotels, the Canadian Pacific and the Sanitarium; the former cost nearly double as much as the latter, but then it is a palace hotel...."

– Douglas Sladen, 1895

"It does no[t] seem fit that one should go into detail on the money or the toil it has cost to bring this

incomparable institution to its present stage of perfection. Mercenary ideas jar the romance of the situation."

Despite the town's pride in the hotel, as well as its dependence upon the hotel for a certain portion of its meal ticket, few of the townspeople ever saw the inside of the hotel, and most were only vaguely aware of the elegant activities which transpired behind the great carved doors. It was very much "a palace unto itself," and very few of the local populace would consider directly transgressing its glittering domain. The concept of social class was a very vigorous doctrine at the turn of the last century and it operated most effectively to keep the "downtown people" downtown.

Yet there were some annual events that tended to bring the hotel and the town into contact with each other on a social plane. The annual hotel summer ball carried the established families of Banff and Calgary briefly into the sequestered realm of the New York and Boston social registers, and lucky guests of the occasions could later speak in casual tones of mingling with European and Eastern royalty.

There were other items, a bit more mundane, which helped to keep the hotel and town in touch. One common problem, which troubled both Banff and the hotel, was that of the penniless transient, a problem which has plagued the better sensibilities of Banff since before the turn of the last century. The transient of 1900 took one of two forms: the common hobo, also known as the boxcar bum (Ross Thompson would have fallen into this category on his 1895 sojourn), or the gentleman thief, the man who would ride the train legitimately in

"Old Jim Stink," one of the early Chinese labourers in Banff.

order to strike up an acquaintance with wealthy travellers and then steal as much of whatever was convenient at the first possible chance.

Both types were anathema to the town. An early news article entitled "The Tramp Nuisance Infesting our Mountain Resorts," decries the presence of such men in Banff: "They must be taught that these sylvan retreats, though free to the world, must be kept absolutely free if not from their presence at any rate from their outrages." At one point the possibility of gentlemen thieves operating at the Banff Springs forced Manager Mathews to ask guests to be most particular with the disposition of their possessions. Both the man in the terraced house and his brother in the streets below discovered that irritation, like love, was a common itch.

Chapter 3

Growing Pains and Capital Gains

"The record of meals served per month at the hotel has exceeded by 2,000 the figure of the great Seattle fair season of two years ago."

By the beginning of the twentieth century, it was apparent that Van Horne's scheme for a string of grand mountain hotels had been a stroke of genius. Within twelve years of its opening, the Banff Springs Hotel had become one of the top two or three mountain resorts on the North American continent, had established a solid international reputation for itself, and was proving to be a lucrative venture for the Canadian Pacific Railway. The Banff Springs was, in fact, famous as a hotel regardless of the mountains.

The 1894 *Baedeker Guide to Canada* listed it as one of the top five hotels in the Dominion (the others were the Chateau Frontenac in Quebec, Windsor Station in Montreal, and Russell House and Grand Union in Ottawa. The guidebook noted that the Banff Springs was particularly noted for its "good cuisine and attendance"). The mountain scenery had indeed been capitalized.

"He will be sure to feel a strong desire to ascend some of the heights, and to gain varied and closer views of many points of scenery that will especially interest him. He will, of course, want to visit the various springs, to cross the Spray, and to walk down the Bow until he can look backward between Tunnel and Rundle Mountains; he will want to study the falls from every accessible point of view, and, taking the little steamer or a canoe, ascend the Bow, push his way into the Vermillion Lakes, and construct for himself varied pictures of the mountains...."

– Bernard McEvoy, 1902

Van Horne had stepped up to the position of the chairman of the board (the company's presidency was now held by Thomas Shaughnessy), and it must have been at least a small source of pride for the man to see requests for hotel additions and improvements flow across the large, polished oak desks of the company's headquarters in Montreal. Such requests were not a small matter. Canadian Pacific Railway hotels, in relation to the number of visitors requiring their services, were shrinking every year. The Banff Springs in particular was experiencing the most severe cramping. The Rocky Mountain Park superintendent's reports to Ottawa for the years 1902-05 reveal the demands with which the hotel was trying to cope: in 1902 hotel guests numbered 3,890; the following year the number of visitors reached 5,303; and in 1904 the number jumped to 9,684. The reports also indicate that during each of those years large numbers of guests were turned away for lack of accommodation.

The Banff Springs Register, which the park superintendent considered some of the best reading material in Banff in 1905, showed on one page names from South Africa, the Hague, Paris, Austria, England, Japan, Canada, the U.S., Borneo and Hong Kong.

In order to meet the demands of an expanding international clientele, the CPR started a program of hotel extension and improvement that fostered an addition or rearrangement in the Banff Springs' structure almost every year between 1900 and 1928, the year in which the present hotel was completed. The 28-year span is neatly divided into two periods: 1900 to 1910, during which all modifications dealt directly with the original 1888 building, and 1910-1928, during which all modifications were directed toward the ultimate end of a "new" hotel.

Exact dates and figures concerning construction at the Banff Springs between 1900 and 1910 are few and far between. The superintendent's reports comment that large additions were made in 1903, 1904, and 1905. Of these additions the most extensive was that of the winter of 1902-03. In 1902 the CPR allocated a half-million dollars for construction and refurnishing. At the end of the summer season a crew of workers began a full winter's work, duplicating the west wing of the original structure on a site just a few feet to the south of the copied wing, giving the hotel the basic north-south orientation it has maintained until today. The two wings were joined by a low split-level wooden passageway.

The Fairmont Algonquin as it looks today.

Canada's Other Railway Hotels

It was an early marketing strategy of the Canadian Pacific Railway to have passengers stay in company-owned hotels. This led to the construction of hotels in prominent city locations and through the remote wilderness penetrated by the transcontinental rail line. Competing railway companies such as the Grand Trunk Railway and Canadian National followed suit. The result was a string of grand hotels stretching from coast to coast, attracting wealthy guests from around the world and, today, forming part of Canada's national identity. In addition to the Banff Springs Hotel, railway companies constructed the following properties:

The Algonquin (St. Andrews, New Brunswick): Opened 1889 and the now the Fairmont Algonquin, this sprawling waterfront resort was built near Van Horne's summer home.

Chateau Champlain (Montreal, Quebec): Opened in 1967 for the World Fair, this former CPR hotel with its distinctive porthole windows is now the part of the Marriott chain.

Chateau Frontenac (Quebec City, Quebec): Expanded many times since 1899, this property now operates as the Fairmont Le Château Frontenac.

Chateau Montebello (Montebello, Quebec): Opened in 1930 as the world's largest log hotel; now Fairmont Le Château Montebello.

Chateau Lake Louise (Banff National Park, Alberta): A chalet built by the CPR in 1890 has grown in stature and form to become one of the world's most photographed hotels.

Château Laurier (Ottawa, Ontario): This popular politico hangout opened in 1912 and is today known as the Fairmont Château Laurier.

The Empress (Victoria, British Columbia): This Edwardian landmark overlooking the Inner Harbour opened 1908 and is now the Fairmont Empress.

Fairmont Empress.

The Fort Garry (Winnipeg, Manitoba): A classic 1913 Chateau-style railway hotel that, like the Banff Springs, is now a National Historic Site.

Glacier House (Glacier National Park, British Columbia): Opened in 1886; closed in 1925.

Hotel Macdonald (Edmonton, Alberta): This 1914 Chateau-style hotel was saved from demolition in the 1980s and is now a treasured part of the Fairmont family.

Hotel Novascotian (Halifax, Nova Scotia): Blending Colonial and Neo-classical styles, this former Canadian National property built in 1928 is now part of the Westin chain.

Hotel Saskatchewan (Regina, Saskatchewan): Open by the CPR in 1927, this Neo-classical downtown property is the city's finest hotel. It is now part of the Radisson chain.

Hotel Vancouver (Vancouver, British Columbia): This copper-roofed 1939 landmark is now the Fairmont Hotel Vancouver.

Jasper Park Lodge (Jasper, Alberta): Originally a row of lakeside tents operated by the Grand Trunk Railway, this upscale resort is now operated under the Fairmont brand.

Minaki Lodge (Minaki, Ontario): Built along the CNR line in 1927, after a checkered history, this resort-style log hotel burnt to the ground in 2003.

Mount Stephen House, Field, around 1900.

Mount Stephen House (Yoho National Park, British Columbia): Opened in 1886 as a dining station and evolving into a hotel, the structure was demolished in 1963.

Palliser Hotel (Calgary, Alberta): Opening in 1914, this landmark hotel was the first CPR property to move away from the Chateau style to Neo-classical. It is now part of the Fairmont chain.

Place Viger Hotel (Montreal, Quebec): Deigned by Bruce Price and incorporating a railway station, this hotel opened in 1898 but closed in 1935. Restored in 2003, it is now a school for tourism.

Queen Elizabeth Hotel (Montreal, Quebec): This landmark hotel of over 1,000 rooms dates to 1958 and is officially known as Fairmont the Queen Elizabeth.

Royal York Hotel (Toronto, Ontario): Flagship of the CPR city hotels, this property opened in 1929 and is now the Fairmont Royal York.

The hotel's new appearance created a local journalistic furor. A news clipping from 1903 claims that one could march an army of 3,000 men into the building. The reporter envisions soldiers five abreast swinging through the south doors and marching down the main hall, leaving yet enough room for an officer to "pass up and down the line without being crowded to the wall." Considering the commotion caused some years later when a slightly inebriated park warden rode his horse into the main lobby of the hotel, it's just as well that no one tried to verify the accuracy of the journalist's claim. It's safe to assume, though, that Manager Mathews was content that his hotel could now house two-thirds again as many as the first hotel's 300 guests. In truth, the closest thing to an army to ever reach the hotel was the celebrated 56th Regiment Iowa National Guard Band of Fort Dodge, Iowa, a great hit at the 1908 summer ball.

As to the interior renovations, it appears that the management continued its previous motif:

"It is finished in native wood – Douglas fir – every piece of which has gone through the hands of artistic wood workers. The ceiling and other decorations have been put on in accord with perfect harmony, and the electric lights—well, thousands have been spent on them. The parlours, the sleeping rooms, retreats, refreshment booths, verandas, baths, and all such are modern and luxurious to the limit."

The 1903 season also witnessed the installation of a complete set of telephones in the hotel, although there had been one phone, one of four in Banff, in the hotel some years earlier. Banff itself was one of the earlier "wired" towns in the west. But even with a new wing, a new interior, and the luxury of telephones, the hotel could no more accommodate the number of guests desiring rooms in 1903 than it could in 1902. The park superintendent's report sums up the problem:

"No less than 5,000 guests were turned away from Banff during the past season. The Banff Springs Hotel was compelled to remain open for a month later than usual owing to its increasing popularity among the travelling public. Notwithstanding the large additions made to the building in 1903, which includes the addition of over 200 rooms, the management has since found it necessary to make arrangements for yet another large addition…"

As a matter of interest, the proposed addition was to be built "with a view to being utilized throughout the winter." Such a theme was a common one in Banff from 1900 until well into the 1920s, with merchants claiming that each succeeding winter would be the winter that would establish Banff as a major winter resort. The Banff Springs Hotel was certainly not immune to the pull of such speculative possibilities, and progressive generations of managers toyed with the idea of making the hotel a year-round resort. Not until 1969 did the hotel open year-round.

"The only business at Banff is to enjoy one's self, to recreate, to loaf in the sunshine and worship nature."

– Bernard McEvoy, 1902

The exact nature of the "large addition" of 1904, or the addition of 1905, is not known for sure, but it is at least possible that during these years two six-story frame towers were constructed, one tower apiece for the north and south wings. With their steep-hipped and dormered roofs, the

A horse-drawn buggy leaving the hotel, 1910.

towers bore a strong resemblance to the ones that occupy similar positions today. There is evidence to suggest the towers were not constructed until a somewhat later date than 1904 and 1905. If they were indeed constructed in those early years, it is more than likely that one of the first guests to enjoy the elevated view provided by the towers was Joe Cannon, the long-time Speaker of the U.S. House of Representatives. Cannon checked into the hotel during the season of 1905 with a large retinue of fellow legislators and their wives. One wonders what "Uncle Joe," who once vowed that the House would spend "not one cent for scenery," thought of the Canadian Rockies.

In 1906, another small luxury item found its place among the steadily growing "comforts" recorded for the Banff Springs when six arc lights were erected along the road to the hotel. No reports indicate popular sentiment concerning this particular innovation, although it does appear that most folks were impressed with the technology of the lights and the very act of erecting the lamps, a problem not made easier by six Italians on the crew who spoke no English.

The alterations continued during the winter of 1906-07, when a crew of some 70 men worked almost continuously to build a new boiler, engine and laundry room. The new addition, at the southeast end of the hotel, was considered unique because it was constructed entirely of river boulders and featured a 90-foot smokestack which, as a news clipping of the day informs us, "it is safe to say will be recorded on many hundreds of photographic films before the season is over."

The only thing that outpaced construction during these years was, again, the number of persons wanting to make use of the construction. There

The Banff Springs Hotel in Print

The earliest direct fictional reference to the Banff Springs Hotel is in a 1910 novel, *Lady Merton, Colonist,* by Mrs. Humphry Ward (also known as May Augusta Ward), a well-known English novelist of the era. It was a story of romantic intrigue, which uses as its major setting the trans-Canadian railway journey. The reference to the hotel is a rather flowery description of the view from the terrace:

"...the hotel at Banff overlooks a wide scene of alp and water. The splendid Bow River comes swirling past the hotel, on its rush from the high mountains to the plains of Saskatchewan. Craggy mountains drop almost to the river's edge on one side; on the other, pine woods mask the railway and the hills; while in the distance shine the snow-peaks of the Rockies."

seemed to be no end to the problem. When the hotel opened in May of 1907 it was promptly filled to capacity with 450 registered guests, the start of another over-flow season. The trend continued in 1908 and 1909, and during the summer of 1910 the hotel sent close to 400 persons back to the railway station to find shelter in sleeping cars at $1.50 per night. During that summer the hotel entertained at least two parties notable enough to make the local paper: a convention of over 100 Winnipeg businessmen; and the Maharaja of Baroda, accompanied by the Maharani, their two children, and an entourage of friends and servants.

And, if the season of 1910 were sublimely busy, the season of 1911 approached the ridiculous. Well over 22,000 persons stayed at the hotel over the course of the summer, and it was noted "the record of meals served per month at the hotel has exceeded by 2,000 the figure of the great Seattle fair season of two years ago." There were two or three dances a week, the tennis courts were full to overflowing every day that the weather permitted, and a golf course saw some 1,500 guests try its greens during the first nine weeks of its existence.

> *"What is the difference between this hotel and the C.P.R.?" asked a grouchy guest at the King Edward recently. "Just a mile, sir," was Tabby's reply, and the humour of it dispelled the grouch.*
>
> – Crag and Canyon, 1907

While the folks downtown fulminated about the growing number of "roughs" in town – the "class of visitor who make the Banff trip as an excuse for a glorious drunk," the Banff Springs was spending a bit of time worrying not about quality but about quantity. The quantity of quality remained the greatest problem the hotel faced.

Chapter 4

Balconies and Towers, Turrets, Time and Troubles

"The Chateaux of the Loire... or is it early William Randolph Hearst?"

By 1910, it was apparent that the piecemeal approach to construction, which the hotel had pursued for the previous decade, could not hope to solve the institution's more pressing problems. Furthermore, the staggering headcount for the 1910 and 1911 seasons, including those persons who had been bedded down at the railway station, emphasized the point that the hotel's potential was falling far short of fulfillment. The well-groomed men of Montreal bent their greying temples together in conference and announced what appeared to be a simple answer—begin work on a new Banff Springs Hotel. And where the old hotel had been the "largest and finest mountain resort on the continent," make the new hotel larger and finer yet.

Whether the planners of 1910 envisioned a completely new structure, one to be built in stages over a number of years, or merely a greatly modified and integrated structure involving the old components, is difficult to determine, but their decision to alter significantly the hotel's appearance and create something "new" was the key element in the evolution of the building which stands today, completed in 1928.

The man commissioned to design the "new" hotel was Walter S. Painter, an American who had been working as the chief architect for the Canadian Pacific Railway since 1905. Painter was acquainted with Banff and the Banff Springs Hotel at the time of the commission, having visited the community in the years before 1911. Indeed, it seems most likely that he was directly involved with much of the Banff Springs development in the years between 1903 and 1911.

As an architect, Painter was influenced by both Price's work and the whole of the CPR chateau tradition, while also to prove himself an able successor to Price's throne (Price had passed away in 1903). The CPR had begun to stray from the chateau style by 1910, especially in its designs for city hotels (such as Calgary's Palliser Hotel, which was completed for the CPR in 1914 in a Neo-classical style), but the chateau was still held to be an appropriate mode for all mountain resorts, and Painter was treated to an extensive tour of the Loire region of France before he began to draw up plans for the new Banff Springs Hotel.

Walter S. Painter, architect of the new hotel.

As a matter of incidental interest, Painter's trip to the Loire poses some intriguing questions for the person interested in the Banff Springs' stylistic origins. Painter spent his summer in the Loire studying and sketching superb examples of the unadulterated French chateau, and then came home to build a structure that is almost entirely lacking in the features that characterize the French medieval style. The dormers of the present hotel are flat rather than pointed; the arches are circular rather than the more pointed Gothic style; and the windows of the centre tower are rounded, features which are more indicative of the Scottish baronial tradition than of the pure French chateau.

The problem has at least two answers. The Scottish baronial style of the sixteenth and seventeenth centuries was heavily influenced by the Loire chateaux, and Painter was probably interested in seeing the original source material. And the CPR was anxious to exploit the well-nurtured (and largely mythic) conception that the Banff of the Canadian Rockies somehow resembled the fishing village of Banff in Scotland. This latter theme has

Painter's sketch for a "new" Banff Springs Hotel. Only the centre tower, however, was completed as sketched. Other plans, designed by J.W. Orrock, were used in constructing new wings 13 years after completion of the tower.

played an important part in the projected image of Banff and the Banff Springs Hotel since the turn of last century, and it has even been speculated that Price's 1888 structure was designed with a Scottish manse in mind. This though is doubtful, and, besides, the original building was much too loose a structure to allow such architectural pinpointing.

At any rate, the hotel, as finished in 1928, is one which owes much architecturally to both the French and Scottish styles but which, in fact, represents an exacting copy of neither. Nor is it, as one visitor has suggested, "early William Randolph Hearst." It is, as was the original hotel, its own building, diverse in influence and rich in design.

The first step in the creation of the new building was taken shortly after the hotel closed at the

Work on the centre tower nears completion in 1912.

end of the 1911 season. A crew of some 200 men started to work at tearing out the existing centre portion of the hotel and preparing foundations for a new reinforced concrete middle wing. The new wing was to become part of an eleven-story centre tower, given advanced billing as the tallest building in the Canadian Rockies.

But most of the work that first winter went toward the completion of the centre tower and the development of two new swimming pools and a series of bathing rooms. The number of men on the job, many of them brought to town by the CPR, gave Banff its "finest winter to date," and the local paper reported happily that the winter sports club and the hockey club were very active all winter. The influx of men also created the first recorded housing shortage in Banff. The work on the wing and the pools was completed by the early spring of 1912, and the finished product gave full support to the notion that the new structure was to be a very grand affair. The pools and baths were particularly impressive. A Calgary newspaper reported that the Banff Springs Hotel opened the season with "the finest bathing establishment on the continent," while the Banff paper mentioned a "general air of luxury" about the place.

The "establishment" consisted of three terraces. The outer and lower one was a semi-circular cold, fresh-water pool, while the second terrace held a warm sulphur pool, 8.5 metres (28 feet) by 24 metres (80 feet), heated to 43 degrees Celsius (110 degrees Fahrenheit), and separated from the outer pool by a graceful loggia (open-sided arcade). The second terrace also contained complete Turkish and Russian baths with no less than 100 individual dressing rooms. The Turkish baths, with marble partitions and walls and floors of imported English tile, proved to be the most popular. They were, sniped a local journalist, "quite the best part of the Dominion," although

Rugged Rundlestone

The hotel's exterior stone is locally quarried Rundlestone (originally known as Rundle rock). The stone is distinctive for its rugged qualities and deep gray, black, and brown hues. In geological terms it is sedimentary shale laid down on an ancient ocean floor 250 million years ago, and as a result traces of fossilized sea life are common. It was first excavated in the 1890s from the base of Mount Rundle (the original quarry is still visible along the Spray River Circuit hiking trail 1.2 km/0.7 miles from the hotel). Today, Rundlestone is excavated at Thunderstone Quarries, near Canmore. This is where stone used in the hotel's most revamp was sourced, and you'll also see it used in fireplaces, rock gardens, and interior floors throughout the mountain towns.

the same fellow complained that "it would be more comfortable in the dressing rooms if there were wooden gratings to stand on instead of the bare concrete floors." The third and final terrace consisted of cooling rooms, private sulphur baths, and rooms for an imported Swedish masseur, while the roof to the third terrace functioned as a wide promenade. All things considered, there was indeed a general air of luxury about the baths.

One of the first people to enjoy the use of the new baths was none other than the Duke of Connaught. The Duke (the brother of King Edward) and Duchess (Princess Louise Margaret Alexandra Victoria Agnes of Prussia) stopped briefly at the hotel on their first Canadian transcontinental journey, and the Duke promised to return, saying "...my only regret is that I have so short a time to enjoy the many attractions which are presented by Banff and its vicinities."

Although construction was halted for the duration of the 1912 season, by mid-September the various hammerings and bangings associated with heavy structural creation could be heard above the roar of the Bow Falls. A crew even larger than the one used in 1911 was employed for the winter work of 1912, some estimates ranging as high as 600 men, although it is doubtful that there were ever more than 400 involved with the hotel at any one time.

The work for the next two winters was clear-cut: build the tallest building in the Canadian Rockies, by hand, before the start of the 1914 season. Walter Painter undertook the contract himself and promised to complete the work in two winter's time, a task most persons considered impossible.

The building process was a slow, arduous, and, by today's standards, dramatic one. Most of the labour was hand labour, and the men had access to none of the ingenious mechanical devices that help modern contractors toss up a 20-storey high-rise in a few months. Tons of materials were hauled by wagon from the railway station to the building site and then pushed and pulled into position by the brute force mustered by the builders. Elaborate scaffolding, the construction of which seems nearly as awesome as the work on the hotel itself, was first erected and then enclosed in planks to give the men some protection from the frigid winter winds and the snow which seemed at times to rise more quickly than the tower. But the work did progress, and within thirteen months the hotel manager was able to announce that the "alterations" were almost complete. Painter, it appeared, would make his impossible contract.

The completed structure, known as the Painter Tower and including the preliminary work of the centre wing, was 60 metres (200 feet) long, 21 meters (70 feet) wide, and eleven stories high—a remarkable achievement, given the times and working conditions of the day. It is even more remarkable that during the entire course of construction only two reported architectural mishaps occurred (although there were no doubt more), neither of which could begin to match the blueprints' about-face of the 1888 construction. The first problem arose when one of the walls (the east wall of the tower) fell a bit out of plumb rather early in its rise. The error was not discovered until the building had reached some five or six stories and then it was too late to start over again. But the awkward angle was not great and the wall

Completed centre tower.

was squared up at that point and the building progressed smoothly upward. Today only the most observant guest will notice the slight jog in the wall as it corrects itself and continues its rise. The other blunder was revealed one afternoon when the building was very near completion. One of the construction foremen called Sam Ward, a joiner on the crew, over to him and, pointing to one of the high dormered windows, asked Sam if he remembered anything about the room behind the window. Sam was unsure and the two of them went to investigate. The mystery began to unravel itself when the two men arrived at the proper spot for an entrance to the room and found nothing but a smooth, finished wall. Sam found a pry bar and, while the foreman inched, drove

Detail of the centre tower.

it between the studs. A room was indeed behind the wall and a crew was called up to put a door into an area that might have been sealed off yet.

Nearly everyone agreed the work on the new tower was superb, but if any one element drew universal acclaim it was the stonework. The CPR, to do things properly, had imported Italian stonecutters and Scottish masons, reputedly the best in the world at their respective jobs, to handle the rock facing on the tower.

The facing consists of Rundle rock limestone (known today as Rundlestone), taken from a quarry a little over one kilometre (0.6 miles) from the hotel. Once quarried, the rock was hauled by wagon to the building site where the masons would do the final shaping and laying of the blocks. This particular job proved to be most tedious, as the sedimentary rock is brittle and tends to split and break easily. But the cutters and masons proved equal to their reputations and, as an observant guest might notice today, the rockwork of the centre tower is of the highest quality—far better than the work done in later years on the two wings. The earlier work is of a consistency and quality that in probability couldn't be duplicated today – even if an organization willing to underwrite the expense of an attempt could be found.

One other architectural aspect of the Painter Tower leads to speculation—the great chunk of bedrock – which forms an integral part of the northern wall of the tower (visible where the tower joins the north wing at the back of the Upper Bow Valley Terrace). It was, of course, an architectural decision to incorporate the bedrock into the wall, probably to save the effort of knocking out a particularly

Hotel Chameleon

The rockwork held a surprise for the people working on the new hotel. It changed colour! The Rundlestone, as quarried, had a bluish-grey tinge to it which changes to a rich brown colour with extended exposure to the sun, and with some incredulity early labourers returned to the hotel after a few years' absence to discover their blue castle turned to brown. Today's visitor can observe the difference between the two shades of rock by standing in front of the new lobby, as pictured, where the addition has a distinctive blue-grey colouring compared to the original building.

The centre tower was built around this chunk of bedrock, which is still visible along the Garden Terrace.

An early Mrs. Reed interior.

resistant piece of rock and to add a fine ornamental touch to the structure. The presence of the rock could certainly be used as a facetious argument against any who might claim that Painter's architecture lacked an "organic" sense. Actually, there is one other piece of bedrock, this piece considerably larger, which was never excavated from the hotel's sub-basement. It was simply walled off and, one would suppose, functions as a rather sturdy support for the floors above it.

The Painter Tower was ready for business when the hotel opened in May of 1914. Over two million dollars had been spent on the tower and the new interior, now emphasizing much wicker furniture. The interior was the work of a Mrs. Hayter Reed, a woman of great talent and energy who was responsible for many of the railway hotels' interiors in the first two decades of the 20th century. She was responsible for the various Banff Springs interiors from 1905, when she and her husband lived in Banff, to the late 1920s.

The new tower included a dining room, a large rotunda that became the central lobby for the hotel (now Rundle Hall), and rooms for over 300 guests. Much of the new public floor space was done in red English tile, still very much in evidence, a feature which has led to the despair of many a bellboy in the intervening years, as the bellboys are responsible for keeping each individual tile outlined with a fresh coat of black paint. The meticulous construction of the building as a whole was not going to be diminished by inattention to the smallest detail of upkeep.

The original lobby of the new hotel, as it looks today.

Chapter 5

A Parade of Princes, Politicians and Patrons

"As happy as grigs, whatever a grig may be."

Although Painter's sketches had provided for two new wings as well as a new tower for the Banff Springs – meaning, in effect, a completely new structure – his part in the construction came to an end with the completion of the centre tower. Upon completion of the tower, the upper echelons of the CPR decided to sit back a bit and see how things ran with the new tower and the two older wings. It was to be fourteen years before the rest of Painter's plans, with major modifications by another architect, were to become a reality of steel, concrete, and rock.

The intervening years were prosperous for the hotel, and successive managements worked diligently to maintain and improve the hotel's established reputation as one of the great luxury resorts on the continent. Over the years the hotel had become more and more of a summer home for a number of the guests, and by 1914 many of the people staying at the hotel were seasoned Banff veterans, with ten or more years of "Springing" to their credit.

The Duke and Duchess of Connaught became seasonal repeats when they returned in August of 1914 for a two-week stay, their entourage occupying 22 rooms of the new tower, with an additional ten rooms for servants' quarters. But if the Duke had regrets about leaving Banff in 1912, he had even greater regrets about departing in 1914. Coming back into Banff after a canoe trip down the Bow River one afternoon, the Duke saw a line of scarlet-clad Mounties standing in rank along the riverbank. His guide, Jim Brewster, heard him say, to no one in particular, "Ah, yes, I expected this." Then he lapsed into a profound silence until they beached the canoe. The Mounties presented him with Great Britain's Declaration of War and instructed him a train was waiting at the railway station. Within a few hours, the Duke found himself steaming east across the prairies, heading toward home.

In the following year another guest had regrets about leaving Banff, but for other reasons. Carrying a light fishing rod and speaking vociferously, the Roughrider President of the United States, Teddy Roosevelt, was in town and staying at the Springs. Banff, it appears, appealed to him:

"I am DEE-LIGHTED with your town. Banff is the centre of all that is beautiful, and this part of the mountains is the Yellowstone Park of Canada. I regret exceedingly my time is so limited as nothing would give me greater pleasure than to spend several weeks catching your justly celebrated mountain trout."

The parade of princes, politicians, and patrons continued unhampered throughout the decade, and in 1920 the hotel expanded its celebrity horizons by entertaining the Hollywood cast of Conceit, starring such greats as Betty Hilburn, Maurice Costello, Hedda Hopper, and William Davidson. It was the first of many movies to be filmed near Banff, and the word spread quickly concerning the Canadian Rockies. Glamorous names associated with the film world began to appear more frequently on the pages of the Banff Springs Register.

The hotel, in the meantime, if not expanding, was keeping itself busy with renovation and

Lew Cody spent time at the hotel while filming The Valley of the Silent Men *in 1922. This scene was shot near Tunnel Mountain Campground.*

innovation. The east wing of the 1888 building, which had served for many years as the dining room and kitchen for the original structure, was torn down in 1915, and some 400 guest rooms were redecorated for the start of the 1916 season. The summer of 1916 also introduced Japanese bellboys and waitresses. A lady journalist was hired to act as a society press agent, her job to chronicle "the arrival and doings of all prominent society people" and to see that such arrivals and doings were distributed to the press throughout North America.

Other alterations occurred during the winter of 1916, when the hotel was allotted $140,000 for the construction of another new boiler house and laundry. Apparently the only thing not altered in some fashion was the telephone service, for one visitor remarked that one had as much chance of reaching the desired party "as winning the pot against a royal flush." Actually, one other complaint was levied against the hotel during the 1914-1920 period, but it did not originate with the guests. The CPR, by virtue of possessing a railroad that ran through the town, the local railway station, and a large hotel, exercised a healthy power of persuasion over the potential visitors to Banff. Simply by advertising the CPR hotels on CPR trains and making sure

In 1920, the entrance to Banff National Park was east of present day Canmore.

A four-horse stagecoach loads for sightseeing in the 1920s.

the CPR carriage held the favoured platform position at the CPR station, the company ensured a capacity level crowd for the Banff Springs Hotel.

The other hotels in town developed resentments toward such lopsided arrangements, and in the summer of 1915 several of the managers arranged a meeting with two CPR officials to air the problem. The company listened to the charges and promised to alter the arrangement (although the Banff Springs would maintain its number one spot) and have literature concerning other accommodation in Banff to be circulated on the trains. Otherwise, they remained adamant the CPR hotel would retain all other "privileges of the platform."

The settlement temporarily soothed most tempers, but in August of 1915 the local newspaper ran an editorial which, while stating it had no particular desire to roast the CPR, presented evidence that someone connected with the CPR in the east was advising railway passengers that the Banff Springs

Hotel was the only hotel in Banff, and that if travellers couldn't get a reservation at the Springs they'd be wise to travel on without stopping. That such advice was dispersed seems without a doubt true. After all, it was "vouched for by residents of unimpeachable integrity." But whether such advice was dispersed maliciously or merely through misinformation seems an open question.

Life at the hotel swept on unaffected. The Duke of Connaught finally managed a full two weeks at the hotel during the summer of 1916, and the castle prepared itself for a decade of gracious living. So gracious, indeed, that when an old-timer named Morley Roberts, who had helped put the railroad through Banff in 1883, returned in 1925 he found the hotel somewhat beyond credulity:

"The truth is that I could not take beautiful Banff seriously. I dreamed it, and like so many dreams it was at once absurd and beautiful. On a pine-covered bank or bluff above the crystal foam of the Bow I came to a gigantic castle. It had no business being there, for when I was thereabouts so long ago no one could have thought of it. It was full of most curious looking people who seemed very busy about nothing at all but were as happy as grigs, whatever a grig may be. They wore all kinds of odd costumes. Some women, so greatly determined on being noticed as to defy ridicule flaunted about in long shining boots and scarlet jackets and jockey caps, while others wore clothes "made in America" in the back woods, which looked as if they had been cut out with an axe. The dream castle was full of such people who talked all at once and I saw in a moment that they were not real. I, or someone else, had imagined them. If any of us workers of the old days had seen their likes we should have thought we had delirium tremens at the least."

Enjoying afternoon tea on the Bow Valley Terrace.

For the guests of the hotel, however, there was no question of reality – life was as socially painful (or ecstatic) as it had ever been. Just as the townspeople conducted their periodic raids on old Jim Toy's Laundry, looking for Chinese Whiskey and opium, so the British guests conducted their periodic raids on the ever-suffering American guests. According to the local paper dated August 12, 1922:

"A newly rich American, a class which is flooding the country just now, approached an English gentleman in the Banff Springs Hotel recently with the query: 'Say, where is the lavatory?' The Englishman coolly looked his questioner over and replied: 'Go down that corridor and turn to the right where you will see a door with the sign Gentlemen on it, but don't let that deter you, old top."

As regular as clockwork, the cycles moved inexorably on through the years.

Chapter 6

Out of the Fire, Its Wings are Stretched

"The level chambers, ready with their pride, were glowing to receive a thousand guests." – John Keats

By 1925, the time had arrived for the completion of the plans begun in 1911. As early as the fall of 1921 the CPR authorized nearly $2 million dollars for the destruction of the old wooden wings of the hotel and their replacement by rock-faced, fireproof structures. The record season of 1922, which saw 400-500 guests registered daily throughout July and August (a grand seasonal tally of some 52,000 visitors), provided a compelling rationale for further expansion.

The new wings would be built over the course of

two years—one to be erected during the winter of 1926-27, and the other the following winter. First it was necessary for a separate annex to be built, a structure that would serve as substitute housing for the regular hotel guests while the wings were being replaced. Accordingly, at the close of the 1925 season, a 100-room building was erected to the south of and below the existing south wing, a structure which, in its grey, cement-finished exterior surface and its decorative allusions to the Tudor style, broke with the rest of the hotel's chateau motif. Now part of what is known as the Manor Wing, the annex today stands as a rather curious Tudor anomaly amidst the other rock-faced Gothic structures that compose the entirety of the hotel.

The work on the annex was completed toward the end of March, 1926, a date which proved to be none too soon. On the sixth of April, 1926, at 11 A.M., the hotel's assistant manager, J. B. Coysh, and a CPR publicity man, Chief B. C. Long Lance, noticed great amounts of smoke curling skyward from the north wing of the hotel. Coysh filed a fire report immediately and within an hour over 500 men were at the hotel, fighting a very businesslike blaze. The old wooden wing burned brightly and rapidly, and by 2 P.M. the last of the original 1888 hotel was a smouldering pile of debris. The firefighters, including some men who raced in from Calgary, far from being able to save the wing, had to be content with rescuing as much furniture as possible and trying to keep the damage to the centre tower at a minimum.

The structure of the centre tower, shielding the south wing from harm, sustained grievous injury itself when a major explosion in the basement blew

A photo taken during the early stages of the 1926 fire. The arches in the foreground can today be seen as part of the pool complex.

out many of the windows and fittings of the tower. And flames crept inside the centre tower to gut the gracious 13-year-old dining room. Flames from the fire struck both the north and west faces of the centre tower, and the smoke-stained surfaces of the tower can be seen today where the new north wing joins the tower on the river side of the hotel (walk onto the Garden Terrace from Rundle Hall and look upwards). The fire itself was attributed to labourers involved in pre-season blasting operations around the base of the north wing, preliminary work for the replacement construction which was to begin at the close of the 1926 season. The workers had built a fire close to the old wing and the flames spread unnoticed to the main building itself.

Rumours at the time suggested a theory that the fire had been set intentionally by workmen under orders from CPR officials, but there is little if any evidence to support that idea. Any such fire would be sure to delay the opening of the hotel, as well as reduce greatly the capacity of the hotel during what promised to be a highly lucrative summer; and the idea that a hotel, any hotel, would risk the adverse publicity of a hotel fire is not very solid thinking. If there were to be a fire, though, it could hardly have happened more fortuitously; unless, of course, it could have happened in the fall of 1926, as the wing was to be torn down at the end of the season, plans and moneys existed for a replacement wing, and the fire occurred well before the start of the tourist season—before any guest had arrived who might have been tragically caught in a midsummer blaze.

Following the fire, the CPR acted with a speed and precision that would have befitted old Van Horne

The North Wing, the last section of the original hotel, lies as a smouldering ruin.

himself. Sir Edward Beatty, now president of the CPR, was on the scene within a matter of days, and it was decided that construction on the new wing would begin immediately. A generous budget of $2 million dollars was allocated for the construction of the wing and the work necessary for the restoration of the centre tower. Work was well underway when the hotel belatedly opened its doors on July 1, 1926.

The man in charge of designing the new wings was John W. Orrock, a CPR engineer, whose ideas were compatible with Painter's. Using the general style of the old wooden wings (to which Painter also paid homage in his 1911 sketches for a new hotel), Orrock penned the final additions to the hotel that stands today, making both the north and south wings much larger than those Painter had drawn, angling the towers of the wings gracefully away from the river. He enlarged the centre tower and modified its roofline, thus tying the earlier structure solidly to the new wings.

The north wing was the first to be replaced, and the work proceeded rapidly, although not so smoothly as one might wish. In October 1926, one man was killed and two others seriously injured when a lift derrick collapsed and a steel beam weighing some 2,500 pounds dropped a full three stories onto the men working below. In February the following year, another accident saw a man badly injured as he looked down an elevator shaft, yelling at a man on the lower floor to send up some tile. His powers of timing or observation, or both, were a bit off and the lift came down on his head from above. Construction humour allowed that Bill lost his head in the excitement of getting the tile laid. In truth, his head remained connected to his body and he survived to work another day. The elevator though, was not to be robbed of its grisly prize, and in May it claimed the life of a man who was trying to grease it, an accident held to be the unfortunate fellow's own fault.

The actual structural work of the north wing followed closely the same general procedure as that which went into the centre tower fourteen years earlier: a steel frame was erected, and then, around the steel, a massive plank cocoon, a shelter for the workmen who continued with the concrete and rock work throughout the winter. In the spring of 1927, less than a year after the great fire, the cocoon fell away and a new limestone wing stretched toward the distant peak of Cascade Mountain.

The work on the north wing was considered typical of CPR construction jobs, exhibiting speed and efficiency in completing a given task, but the work on the south wing was even faster. The old wing was torn down at the close of the 1926 season, but construction on the new wing did not begin until the end of the 1927 season, in September. Seven months later, in April 1928, the south wing emerged from its plank cocoon. If this feat were not phenomenal in itself, the crew also found time to extend and rebuild the inner and outer swimming pools, enclosing the inner pool (thus necessitating a switch to non-sulphured waters for the inner pool to avoid gassing the entire hotel).

The swift pace with which the work proceeded (again, as in the 1911-14 period, largely without mechanical aid) insured the hotel would be in readiness for the start of the 1928 season. As spring yielded to summer, people throughout North

A plank cocoon allowed construction to continue on the North Wing through the winter of 1926/27.

America and Europe learned that for the second time in 15 years a "new" Banff Springs Hotel was awaiting their arrival. An inspection team from the CPR, headed by none other than Sir Edward himself, was on hand for the opening ceremonies of the 1928 Banff Springs, the hotel that stands today.

Incidentally, Sir Edward Beatty, president of the CPR from 1918 until his death in 1943, and his crew were none too early for their inspection tour that spring, for it seems that whenever he turned his back, a carpenter or mason would appear from some dark corner to put a quick finishing touch on some not quite completed portion of the hotel. Such activities were discreetly undertaken and kept as distant as possible from

Looking down on the construction of the South Wing from Sulphur Mountain in 1926.

Sir Edward, as he had been promised the hotel would be "finished" upon his arrival. Much to the credit of the workmen, Beatty never did learn of their secretive hammering and polishing.

Nor did he ever learn of a sealed-off room that still stands dark and empty somewhere at the junction of the north wing and the centre tower. The man who sealed off the room could not exactly remember where it is and, unlike the sealed room in the centre tower, this one has no window to offer any clue of its mute existence.

But if Beatty had been surprised to learn of a "dead" room in the hotel, he would have been even more surprised to learn his company had financed the construction of two private residences in Banff. It seems that one of the men carting construction supplies from the railway station to the hotel had a chronic problem keeping a full load on his wagon. Part of each shipment fell off at a particular spot along the route and he never managed to get it all back on. That the lost materials miraculously arose from the dust en route to form two pleasant houses was another secret Beatty never learned. Beatty did learn, however, that highly polished oak floors can be slippery and, recovering his balance and his dignity after a near tumble in the Alhambra Dining Room (which had originally been planned as a ballroom), he ordered the entire floor, so painstakingly and expensively finished, be carpeted immediately.

On the whole, though, Beatty found the hotel much to his liking. If the original hotel had been a place of elegance and refinement, the new hotel was one of haughty grandeur. It was, in short, one of the most beautifully and carefully finished buildings on the continent, and no expense had been spared to make it so. The external appearance of the hotel, despite different building periods and architects, presented a homogenous appearance. Its style ultimately its own, although the Scottish (and thus, implicitly, French) influence is not to be denied. And the hotel still exhibited those features that Bruce Price considered essential for a northern building—massive wall surfaces and steep roofs.

The interior elements of the hotel, on the other hand, were as mismatched as the exterior elements were matched. Still today, the various styles discovered within the building complement each other and even add richness to the hotel's atmosphere, which might be lacking were the interior consistent throughout. Furthermore, the disparate elements reflect, to a certain extent, the nature of the great European castles where succeeding owners would alter portions of the manse to fit their own tastes and the changing styles of the times.

But perhaps even more fascinating than the different styles encountered within the various rooms of the hotel is the lavish and detailed presentation of the styles. In keeping with Banff Springs tradition, the CPR spared no expense in the decoration of the new hotel. In order to enhance the Spanish motif of the Alhambra Room, which served as the hotel's formal dining room until 1972, the company had the great bronze doors that now grace its entrance wrought at a cost of $30,000. For the eight arched windows that provide the "million dollar view" from the Riverview Lounge, the company brought glass across the continent in a custom-fitted boxcar.

Fossil Hunting

The mottled Tyndall limestone used in some hotel stairways and fireplaces constitutes a particularly unusual feature of the Banff Springs Hotel. The stone is heavily fossilized with ancient marine life, including corals, brachiopods, gastropods, cephalopods, snails, nautiloids, and trilobites. In places where the rock has been worn, such as on the circular stairway near the Alhambra Room, it takes on a special lustre and the fossils stand out in high relief. The overall effect is most intriguing. As a guest discovered while listening to a concert in Mount Stephen Hall: *"A strange emotion comes over one who traces with his finger a fossilized trilobite on a windowsill while listening to the music of a modern orchestra."* A good place to admire fossils is in Rundle Hall, on the third stair from the bottom of the stairway leading up to Mezzanine Level 1. (Limestone containing most prominent fossils was placed on the lower stairs, allowing those who stop to admire them can do so from the safety of floor level).

Bedford lime flagstones were shipped in for the floor of Mount Stephen Hall, and for certain decorative work company imported fossil-filled Tyndall limestone from Garson, Manitoba.

The company, of course, was determined to have workmanship commensurate with the quality of the imported materials, and officials demanded that the greatest care be exhibited in the execution of the smallest decorative detail. The oak wainscoting, the linenfold (wood or stone carved to depict folded linen) work, the animal carvings, the delicate plasterwork of the ceilings (an especially beautiful example is the mushroom ceiling of the circular stairway near the Alhambra Room), the highly polished terrazzo floors, the stained glass work, the great carved oak beams of Mount Stephen Hall, and the numerous and varied gargoyles which peer at unsuspecting guests from dark corners—all exhibit a patience and devotion to fine craftsmanship which has all but disappeared in the modern era of plastic imitation, prefabrication, and automation. As one staff member takes pride in pointing out, even the radiator covers are minor masterpieces.

The furnishing of the "new" hotel, a feature of the Banff Springs which today draws as much comment as the general architecture of the building, is a major factor in creating the rich, textured baronial atmosphere of the hotel. The tapestries, prints, rugs and furniture pieces were selected by Michael Delahanty, a former manager of the hotel, and Kate Treleaven, a personal secretary to Sir Edward Beatty. The Leonardo Society of Montreal also helped with the reproduction selection. The elements comprising the present interior were chosen in tandem with the 1927-28 construction and the new decor was presented in its entirety for the first time with the hotel's opening in 1928.

The furniture itself, representing an even greater variety of styles and periods than the interior architecture, was made by the Montreal firm of Castle & Son Manufacturing, and all pieces are exact reproductions of original period furniture. The reproduction work is, in fact, so precise that the plane marks on the original surfaces are exhibited in the reproductions (look for examples on the table in the centre of Mt. Stephen Hall). The pieces chosen for reproduction were found in various European castles and manors, many of the articles reputedly coming from castles and manses near Banff in Scotland.

Many of the prints that grace the walls of the hotel are Gothic and Renaissance in origin and are certainly in keeping with the general milieu of the great halls. It is interesting to note, though, that during the 1930s some of the prints in private rooms were often discovered turned face-to-the-wall or were taken down completely—they were simply too sombre for some of the guests. One painting, depicting an Ontario forest scene, is particular interesting. Not so much for the subject, but for the artist's signature. Painted by William Van Horne in 1903, the railway man drew his signature backwards, a quirk that some suggest was a subtle reference to the original hotel being built the wrong way around. You can see this work hanging in Mount Stephen Hall.

The hotel prides itself on its wide selection of furniture pieces, oriental rugs, and excellent prints, and it maintains a large workshop with a full-

Mount Stephen Hall is as grand today as when it opened in the 1920s.

time staff to keep the pieces in good repair. At one time the hotel kept a "furniture blueprint" of all the public spaces in the building—plans which showed exactly where each piece of furniture, mirror, print and rug was to be placed and kept.

All in all, the hotel, as opened in 1928, exhibited quite a profusion of disparate styles and objects, large and small, which, by virtue of their good taste and excellent craftsmanship, managed to fall together to create a great and feudal atmosphere—a scene set beautifully for the most exciting era the hotel was ever to know.

CANADIAN PACIFIC
Banff
IN THE
CANADIAN ROCKIES

Chapter 7

Of a Brief But Golden Moment

"Who are they, these butterfly ladies in their Paris gowns?"

In the long and glittering history of the Banff Springs Hotel, one era is particularly dazzling, that span of time stretching from the completion of the "new" hotel to the outbreak of World War II. During this period of the late 1920s and 30s, the hotel seemed to achieve a perfect blend of the realities of day-to-day hotel life and all the preconceived fantasies one might hold of life at a luxury hotel—the reality and the myth fused and became one and the same. Not that anything much had changed from the earlier days, at least on a superficial level. Princes and politicians

The Banff Springs Hotel as it looked in a 1930 postcard.

still frequented the halls, money flowed easily through familiar hands, the traditions of the hotel remained the same, and comments made concerning the hotel carried the same tenor in 1937 as in 1897. Indeed, just as a prominent New York journalist could claim in 1909 that:

"Between New York and Shanghai... there is no spot more cosmopolitan than the rotunda of the C.P. Hotel at Banff.... The women in this group of people in the rotunda of the hotel are dressed as attractively as any women in any hotel in the world, and when the orchestra plays and the people move about talking to each other I could imagine myself in Buenos Aires, in Bombay, in Melbourne, in Malta, in Cape Town or in any other city in which the currents of the world come together."

So could a London writer exclaim in 1937:

"Of one or two places in the world it has been said that if we would but bide there a while we would see all our friends, in due course, pass by. Of such and such

a chair at the Café de la Paix in Paris that has been said, and of the Strand Corner, in London, by Charing Cross. To the number of these places I would add the Banff Springs Hotel. Sit in the portico there, and in due time all your old friendships will be renewed."

But there was, somehow, a difference between that earlier pre-WWI era, characterized by the brisk and measured step of propriety, and the *entre deux guerres* era, perhaps best characterized by the phrase "cultured ease," which found its fullest expression in the 1930s. The change in general attitude registered at the hotel, though, was a reflection of changes in the world at large. World War I dealt a crushing blow to the moneyed classes of Europe, who, in high Victorian idealism, considered themselves responsible for, and in control of, the ebb and flow of the world's fortunes. Such an image of importance pointed toward a logical social conclusion of great emphasis on personal propriety—one had to wear the responsibilities of one's money in an exemplary fashion. The war was not a pretty one; and the self-congratulatory esteem of the wealthy classes disappeared in the dark smoke hanging over the Marne, Vimy Ridge, and Ypres. At the armistice little was left of the previous

---

Where have they been all day, these butterfly ladies who flutter around the hotel at night in Paris gowns? Riding the trails and roaming the forests in strictly utilitarian togs. After sundown they revert to type, chattering over Banff's smart frocks, whispering over newly met "hims," in this purely feminine retreat. Women especially delight in Banff's refinements of service, its exquisite linens and china, finer than in many wealthy homes. Another purely feminine joy is the beauty parlor where some of the smartest women in the world are skillfully attended.

– from a 1920s Canadian Pacific Railway brochure

---

social tradition, and a new and significantly broader-based social stratification emerged from the crumbled and shattered ways of life.

More important than the breakdown of the social structure was the breakdown of the concepts that accompanied it. The rich and socially ranked people of the world (from which the Banff Springs drew much of its clientele) began to view themselves and their money in a new light, and they began to effect an escape from what had been thought the responsibilities implicit in wealth. The whale-boned Gibson Girl gave way to the casual flapper of the 1920s and the vamp of the 1930s. The collar was being loosened.

In time, the depression played its role. For many people, the uncertainty of the future forced them into contact with the present for the first time, and their conclusion was that they had better live as fully as possible today.

If the Banff Springs, in its broadest institutional interpretation (including its general milieu as well as its physical structure), had been a "sumptuous affair" at the turn of the 20th century, it was, by 1930, just a bit more than "sumptuous," and where it had been "daring" in previous years, it now became "truly extravagant." It was against this general setting that many of the most interesting, most amusing, and most warmly human events in the hotel's history occurred. The hotel vibrated with the quirks and idiosyncrasies which only great wealth can afford, of those social amenities that come only through a coin-clanking upbringing. It was a time of elegant dress, elegant entertainment, and elegant relationships.

It was a time when people would arrive at the hotel with letters of credit worth $50,000, a sum earmarked specifically for a 60 to 90 day stay in Banff. "The men," reports an old banker, "would fish and play golf, and the women would change their clothes." There was a staff of ten porters who did nothing but carry luggage from the station to the hotel and back again, and the hotel had to install a special elevator to handle the huge steamer trunks that arrived like herds of buffalo.

It was also a time when the facade of highbrow snobbishness was stretched dangerously thin across a bubbling cauldron of exuberance. Many of the old-time seasonals undoubtedly preferred the more stolid propriety of the pre-war era and certainly lived their lives to that end, but it must have been hard for them to ignore the shrieks of the young New York debutante who, having declared her boredom with life at the hotel, found herself airborne in the direction of the swimming pool, $300 gown and all.

It's also probable that Murray Adaskin, violinist for the Toronto Trio (and later one of Canada's foremost composers), gained a certain "highbrow"

The Toronto Trio (from left to right, Murray Adaskin, Louis Crerar, and Cornelius Ysselstyn) played 11 seasons at the hotel from 1930 to 1941

perspective the first night the Trio performed at the hotel. The task of the evening was to play for the dinner hour first, and then to give an hour-long concert in the Mount Stephen Hall. As the dinner hour approached, Murray was notified the Trio was not to play in the dining room itself, but in the foyer to the dining room, and that the volume of the music was to be more *piano* than *forte*. Although a bit taken aback by such curious instructions, the Trio accepted their fate and played gracefully and well throughout the dinner hour. It was not until the hotel manager and his wife emerged from the dining room that the musicians began to understand the motivations behind the directives given them. Approaching the young violinist, the manager smiled and then whispered in his ear: "Just fine, Murray—didn't bother a soul!"

But if the manager weren't able to appreciate fully the Trio's music for what it was, there were many who could. The Mount Stephen concerts, presented six nights a week (on the seventh night a local naturalist and author, Dan McCowan, gave a nature talk), were always well received by a discriminating and knowledgeable audience. Many of the members of the New York and Boston fine arts elite would spend their summers at the hotel, and for more than one season Adaskin had his programs examined and edited daily by a Mrs. Hall, a prominent patron of the Boston Symphony.

The arts did, in fact, play a vital role in creating and maintaining the hotel's image. Under the auspices of John Murray Gibbon, a CPR promotion man whose energies and interests seem to have approached the span of those of William Van Horne, the Light Opera Company of Alfred

Heather presented two operas a week throughout the summer seasons of 1930-32. Staged in the Cascade Ballroom, the operas featured many of the well-known singers of the day—Randolph Crowes, Enid Gray, Frances James, and Allan Burt.

Gibbon also introduced a scheme whereby well known artists—such men as Carl Rungius and Walter J. Phillips—were asked to visit the hotel and paint the "Canadian Pacific Rockies."' The plan worked well, providing both the hotel and the artists with excellent publicity, although there is one memorable occasion when things got a little out of hand. One day in 1931, Carl Rungius curtly dismissed from his presence a young man whom he took to be one of the Japanese bellboys. Carl was making final preparations for a show of four local artists—Rungius, Charlie Beil, Nick Grandmaison, and Peter Whyte—which was to open that afternoon. He was simply not about to be distracted from his work by any requests from hotel staff. Only later did Rungius learn the man had been an emissary from the Queen of Siam, then visiting the hotel, who wanted to ask for a special showing for the Queen. The Queen never did visit the show.

But the emphasis on the arts was merely a sidelight, a rich embellishment, to what the hotel had always been—a top rate mountain resort. Pack trips were more popular than ever, a combination of CPR and government money was developing new hiking trails throughout the mountain parks, and by 1930 the CPR had developed a number of backcountry cabins for people to use as overnight shelters on extended trips into the mountains with the Trail Riders of the Canadian Rockies. Climbing, fishing and

TRAIL RIDERS OF THE CANADIAN ROCKIES

In 1923, an eclectic group of outdoor enthusiasts came up with the idea of an organized horseback ride to help promote the Canadian Rockies. Partly for personal reasons, partly for Banff Springs Hotel publicity, CPR promotion man John Murray Gibbon agreed to sponsor the event under the name Order of the Trail Riders of the Canadian Rockies. The committee behind the inaugural ride included such luminaries as Dr. Charles D. Walcott, secretary of the Smithsonian Institute; W.T. Hornaday, director of the New York Zoological Society; and noted wildlife artist Carl Rungius. Also included were Banff locals Mary Schâffer, Jim and Bill Brewster, and Jim Simpson. In that first year, the gathering was held in the Yoho Valley, with over 200 riders camping in tepees, enjoying hearty camp cooking, and listening to music from a piano that was carried into the camp on horseback.

The Trail Riders of the Canadian Rockies continues to thrive to this day, now as a non-profit group organizing 12 rides of between four and six days each summer. Anyone is welcome to join the fun, which includes the use of a horse and experienced guide, all meals, western-style entertainment, and tepee accommodation at a base camp.

Understanding that not everyone was comfortable on horseback, Gibbon established the Skyline Hikers of the Canadian Rockies in 1933. Like the Trail Riders, this organization continues to flourish. Backcountry enthusiasts from around the world gather to enjoy five days of backcountry adventures from a base camp that changes location each year.

canoeing remained popular activities, and golf and tennis were played by the slope of Mount Rundle.

Two other activities associated with the hotel reached special prominence during the "golden era." One was Banff Indian Days, an institution already some 40 years old by 1930, and the other was the Banff Highland Gathering and Scottish Music Festival, a comparatively young but very popular Scottish celebration. From humble beginnings in 1889, Banff Indian Days had grown into a grand celebration in the best tradition of the old West. One year, Helen Keller visited the Banff Springs during the course of the midsummer festival, and the Stoney paid tribute to the great lady by making her an honorary princess of their tribe. The other summer festival, usually held in mid-August, was the Highland Gathering. Initiated by the CPR in 1927, the Gathering became somewhat of an annual national event before it faded away in the mid-thirties. The program notes for the 1931 Gathering provide a little of the flavour of the occasion:

"... when the Highland Gathering [came] to Banff, the Scots of Western Canada rolled up in their thousands to attend and take part, the pipes skirled, the dancers danced, and kilts swung and there was a brave array of tartans in the forest clearing under the serrated peaks of these grim, gray Rockies."

There was a wide variety of competitions—dances that included the Highland Fling, the Seann Triubhas, the Sword Dance, the Scottish Reel, and the Sailor's Hornpipe; regimental piping; highland dress; and Caledonian athletics such as running races, hurdles, discus, javelin, pole vaulting, hammer-throwing, and caber-tossing. Most of the events took place below the hotel, near the tennis courts. The Highland Gathering was unable to sustain itself for more than a decade, though most of the old guests and townspeople remembered it with a special fondness for many years. The demise of the Gathering has been attributed to the frugal nature of the Scots, who, while enjoying the festivities at the Banff Springs, preferred to save their pennies by taking lodging at the downtown hotels.

Banff Indian Days and the Highland Gathering were events of a different nature, but they did hold one thing in common—CPR promotion and money. The late 1920s and '30s represented an era when the hotel's propensity for extravagance was equal to that of the most extravagant guests. The golf course, for example, once again under hotel management, was considered one of the toughest courses on the continent and featured a special imported southern grass (which proved very popular with the local elk). And in 1941, management decided that the horse trail near the hotel was a bit too dusty, so 400 tons of oak bark was imported from Ontario to provide a ten-foot wide, six-km (four-mile) long trail, which was promptly dubbed "Rotten Row" in honour of London's famous equestrian grounds.

Nor did the "special touches" end with silent, dustless trails. In the late 1930s, jazz musician Benny Goodman wrote to say he'd like to visit the hotel, but could do so only if there were a place to land his plane. The CPR arranged to have a landing strip cleared at the base of Cascade Mountain. Goodman did fly in and most of the town turned out to see the first plane landing

BANFF INDIAN DAYS

This local event had its beginnings in 1889, when an extended period of bad weather washed out several railway bridges in British Columbia and all train traffic was halted in Banff. Staff at the Banff Springs Hotel, trying to think up new entertainments for marooned travellers, called on outfitter Tom Wilson to gather members of the local Stoney tribe, who put on an impromptu dance demonstration. The event proved so popular with both the hotel visitors and the townsfolk that it became an annual affair. The highlight was a parade, which began from a gathering point known as the "Indian Grounds," then proceeded along Banff Avenue and across the Bow River to the courtyard of the hotel. The colourful parade marked the beginning of several days of singing, dancing and native athletic competitions. After almost 90 years, the last Indian Days was held in 1978.

In July 2004, the Stoney/Nakoda people returned to the mountains, holding a gathering at what Banff locals still call the Indian Grounds, on the northeast side of downtown between Banff Avenue and the railway line. Very different from the past, this annual event is now a low-key, private gathering where cultural traditions are passed on to a younger generation of First Nations.

ever witnessed in Banff. Goodman was only one of a great number of celebrities to visit the hotel during the golden years. Jack Benny used American silver dollars for tips around the hotel, which was about the best type of tip available in those days. Mickey Rooney, then involved in the Andy Hardy series, was turned down by some unsuspecting debutante when he asked her to dance. Cole Porter, Gracie Fields, Henry Fonda—the list was endless—were other well-known names who found time to spend a day or a week at the hotel.

The 1930s were the hey-day of press-agentry, that particularly zany (and successful) type of promotion which saw starlets sitting on blocks of ice during hot weather or attempting to drive a golf ball with a 25-foot club while standing on the back of an elephant. The idea was to provide such an offbeat or topical photograph that the major news

This photo of actress Ginger Rogers sketching a Stoney Chief was typical of the eye-catching images used to promote the hotel in the 1930s.

services would run the picture, thus advertising either the personality or the place that desired the publicity. In the case of the Banff Springs Hotel, the personality and the place usually worked together, and one discovers photographs of the late Tommie Tweed, a well-known radio actor and dramatist, playing the Banff Springs Golf Course while dressed in a suit of armour, and Ginger Rogers posing prettily and sketching a Stoney chief.

The motion picture industry also provided some publicity for the hotel when it was decided that the building would be the backdrop for the dramatic capture of three escaped Nazis in the filming of *The Forty-Ninth Parallel,* an anti-German effort which somehow managed to plunk several of the Führer's disciples into the middle of the Bow River.

Yet another sort of publicity was gained for the hotel and the Banff environs when James Ramsey Ullman, the well-known writer of mountaineering tales, spent his first honeymoon at the hotel in 1927. A certain amount of his stay was devoted to climbing the peaks near Lake Louise with Rudolph Aemmer, one of the Swiss guides in the area, and from his experiences with Aemmer he wrote *The White Tower.*

The most entertaining moments at the hotel didn't always involve well-known entertainment celebrities. A particular Maharaja, it seems, arrived at the hotel one summer during the mid-1930s with an entourage of some 30 persons. He rented two or three of the larger suites and made clear his intentions of making his stay a lavish epic. The staff didn't blink a collective eye when he ordered two double beds be pushed together, but there was a certain amount of circulated amusement when it was discovered that the potentate was using the two beds solely for his own comfort and his various women were left to sleep on the floor.

During the course of the Maharaja's visit, it was discovered that the lock on the royal jewel box had become jammed and couldn't be opened. The hotel sent up one of the electricians to see if he could do anything to remedy the problem. The worker found the box to be a most beautiful one, inlaid with gems and jewels, but he also found that the lock on the box was a very cheap one—the sort that could be opened with a bobby pin. Realizing that if he opened the box at once it would probably be taken away from him before he got a chance to peek inside, the amateur locksmith pretended to have difficulty with the lock, hoping that the assembled throng of onlookers would eventually lose interest and drift away. The ploy worked and he found himself alone with the box. Quickly opening the lock he lifted the lid and peered inside. The contents were somewhat less than he expected, for at the bottom of the beautifully finished container lay a single rumpled copy of the *Calcutta Racing News*.

Another distinguished and frequent hotel visitor was the Prince of Wales, later Edward VIII. The Prince was particularly fond of Alberta—so much so that he bought a ranch south of Calgary and would spend as much time as possible there each year. He also spent a fair amount of time in Banff and the mountainous environs, and it is rumoured each local girl knew somewhere in her heart of hearts she was the proper woman for the royal bachelor. But, alas, it was a matter

King George VI and Queen Elizabeth with Prime Minister William Lyon Mackenzie King on a 1939 hotel visit.

of royal blood, and royal blood was in short supply in the villages of the Canadian Rockies.

In May of 1939, King George VI and Queen Elizabeth stopped in Banff on their transcontinental tour. Canada's prime minister, William Lyon Mackenzie King, was with them, filling out the most important triumvirate ever to visit the hotel. The King and Queen and their entourage had the entire hotel to themselves for two days, and the management was able to concentrate its considerable administrative abilities on the couple. One of the special touches featured by the hotel for their visit was the distribution of huge bouquets of wildflowers throughout the building, something the Queen took special note of. The couple proved to be as genteel as royal tradition requires, and gracefully consented to stop in and have tea at the home of their Banff chauffeur, Jim Brewster. It is a matter of some local historical humour that Jim failed to notify his wife he was bringing the King and Queen.

There were other, earthier, guests. Most of the staff that worked at the hotel through the 1930s remembers a certain Miss Steele, an old spinster who was perhaps more eccentric even than the Maharaja but who didn't rate the social insularity provided by a foreign birth. Miss Steele used to arrive at the hotel every summer with yards and yards of two-inch medical tape with which she would promptly seal off all the windows and doors to her room. This was evidently to prevent any stray wisp of smoke from drifting into her room. Cigarette smokers, she was sure, were trying to poison her. In the dining room she would take her meals in a distant corner and if anyone who had the slightest appearance of being a smoker chose to sit at an adjoining table she would immediately move to some other distant corner. Although quite wealthy, she made a habit of wearing an old brown coat around the hotel which, to put it mildly, was well worn. She finally joined the Banff Springs Hall of Infamy one summer by leaving a small bag of candies as a tip for the girl who had looked after her hermetically sealed room all season. "But I wouldn't eat them, dear," she told the girl, presenting her with the rumpled brown paper bag, "I think they've got worms in them."

Luckier than the young housekeeper was one of the drivers for the Brewster Company, the local transport outfit that has enjoyed a long and close relationship with the hotel. As a Brewster driver, the young man was hired by one of the hotel guests, a middle-aged and wealthy woman, to be her personal chauffeur for the summer. The woman became quite fond of the driver and at the season's end asked him if he wouldn't drive her home to San Francisco. The fellow agreed and the two of them left for California. At the trip's end she reluctantly said goodbye and presented him with a token of her esteem—a cheque made out for $1,500, a sum, she said, which was to go toward his college education.

The hotel has always managed to deal with the idiosyncrasies of wealth in good fashion. When a Doctor Fowler from New York demanded that he be provided with fresh goat's milk at mealtime, a goat was bought and tethered at the back of the hotel and one of the busboys was appointed the official milker. And it was taken as a matter of fact (and usually interest) that every Saturday night someone would try on the suit of armour that used to stand at the bottom of the staircase near the ballrooms—the staff became quite habituated to the sound of an errant knight in his cups ricocheting down the dimly lit corridors.

The staff itself in those days was a strictly professional outfit, and the same people who worked the Banff Springs in the summer would spend the winters at the great resorts in California, Hawaii, Bermuda, and Florida. As might be expected with professionals, the staff was highly efficient (although they might have denied it at the time) and, as the depression wore on, increasingly dedicated to their jobs.

One of the best remembered of the golden years' staff was a diminutive but charming maître d' named Oscar Wulliman, a man seemingly predestined to serve the calling of the great dining rooms of the continent. He did, in fact, prove to be such an excellent servant that the King of Siam insisted that Oscar accompany him as his personal waiter to Victoria, and then he tried to engage him on a permanent basis. Wulliman, however, declined the offer and returned to Banff. Oscar's dedication to the hotel and to the cause of elegant dining was demonstrated more fully at a later date when he was serving a private dinner party for the visiting Reynolds (of Reynolds Tobacco fame) family. Mr. Reynolds had caught a prize trout and, in the usual hotel tradition, it was exhibited during the day in the hotel lobby. That night the fish was stuffed, garnished, and baked to order and Wulliman entered the dining room with the fish held high on a silver platter. But, as fate would have it, someone had dropped a pat of butter on one of the two steps leading into the room and, as happens once in every waiter's life, Wulliman and the fish went down together. To the sound of some not-so-polite snickers, Oscar pieced the fish together and proceeded to the Reynold's table where he served the meal as best he could with one arm – the other had been broken in the fall!

Another well-remembered staff member is a chef named Robert. Robert was as evil-tempered and spiteful as Oscar was polite and charming. In the true chef's tradition, he threw pots and pans around the kitchen, hurled carving knives at helpers, and, one day, reaped all that he had sown. Walking past the still room (the area where the specialty items, such as fancy desserts, were prepared) one evening toward the end of the season, Robert made some passing comment to a young female helper who was doing something on the far side of a long

A group of nuns painting the hotel from Surprise Corner.

counter which ran the length of the room. The girl made some flippant reply (the exact nature of the conversation is now long lost) and Robert exploded. Brandishing a large spoon he leapt into the room and vaulted over the top of the counter—to land with great ceremony right in the middle of 360 dessert dishes of jello, each topped with whipped cream and one-quarter of a maraschino cherry.

There were also, upon occasion, certain administrative mishaps. An over-anxious front desk clerk one year managed to check the first two parties of the season into the same room, a *faux pas* known in the trade as "double-rooming." And at the end of the same year, after the staff had carefully checked out the last of the guests, someone discovered a fellow sleeping soundly in a laundry room, the victim of certain excesses indulged in at the hotel's closing ceremony the night before. He had been overlooked in the general rush to close the hotel. Despite such occurrences, however, the hotel did well manage to maintain its atmosphere of cultured decorum. Proper dress for the evening concerts and dances was full formal attire, and no one would dare approach the dining room without a tie and jacket. No less a personage than Lady Duff Cooper, the wife of a prominent British politician, was refused entrance to the Alhambra Dining Room when she appeared at the door one day in her blue jeans, just back from a long trip on the trail.

There was one spot, though, where Lady Cooper would have been more than welcome in whatever

The Cascade Ballroom was a social hub for guests in the 1930s.

she chose to wear. There was, where the hotel's parkade is today, a small Chinese restaurant known as Sam's Place. It was officially a restaurant for Brewster packers and drivers, but unofficially it served as a common meeting ground for not only Brewster cowboys but hotel staff and guests as well. It became, in time, as much a part of the hotel experience as the evening dance. Sam's was known as *the place* for anyone interested in having a good meal and a good time after the hotel's kitchens closed for the evening, and 11 P.M. on any given summer's evening would find the small building packed with a wide and interesting assortment of folks. Cowboys well into their cups could go through their routines with an eye on the brunette debutante in the corner, and the suave young men in tuxedos could at last put their elbows on the counter and talk to the chambermaids.

By 1940, the impact of World War II was being felt throughout Canada, and Banff, as a resort town, equated its well-being with the well-being of the nation. For the Banff Springs Hotel, the war meant the loss of its European patronage, and restrictions on money and travel hindered North American travel as well. By 1942 it was decided that the hotel would close its doors for the duration of the war. With the closing of the doors came the end of the greatest era in the hotel's history, a time rich in the counterpoint of stiff Victorian propriety and that new sort of life which saw young women protesting a bit too much as young men dragged them toward the pool. The grand halls, now empty, echoed not only the soothing strains of a Mozart trio but the sound of the eternal drunk in the knight's outfit as well. The life of great glitter was over, perhaps never to be recaptured in quite the same spirit.

Chapter 8

Tours and Tribulations: An Age of Transition

"A grand old hotel wending its way through the age of Aquarius."

In the years following World War II, the Banff Springs Hotel underwent a rather significant change, orienting itself toward the demands of modern economics and a broadly social based clientele. The trend was noticeable in the years just prior to the closing of the establishment in 1942, when the hotel began to cater to large numbers of people associated with regularly scheduled train tours. Such tours, quite moderate in price, originated in the large cities of eastern Canada and operated on an itinerary that generally allowed for a night or two in Banff at the Banff Springs Hotel. The popularization of these tours broke the tradition of the well-heeled long-term guests as the "ruling class" of the hotel. Just as the social aftermath of World War I led to a clientele composed of a broader base, so did the combined factors of greater mobility and a popularization of prices between the two world wars point toward an even greater extension in the social base.

A 1942 aerial view of the Banff Springs Hotel.

World War II and its accompanying economic boom in North America completed what was begun before the war. More North Americans owned cars than ever before. Roads were getting better every year and many of them, it seems, led to the Banff Springs (although, as one weary jaded guest pointed out, "just as many of them lead away"). Mobility, accessibility, and the general availability of money functioned together to change the entire context of the hotel experience. The old clientele, to be sure, still visited the hotel, spending their summer at the Banff Springs and the Chateau Lake Louise, and the celebrities still flocked to

A 1940s CPR advertisement for the hotel.

the hotel—many people remember the bellboys fighting among themselves to see who would push Marilyn Monroe around in her wheelchair after she twisted her ankle filming the 1954 hit *River of No Return*—but a higher percentage of each succeeding year's total revenue was coming from the short-stay, tour-scheduled guest.

In due time, the hotel found a majority of its guests was of the upper-middle class, rather than the straight upper, and, in keeping with the times, it began to relax its previous customs of formality. Dress for concert and dance slipped from formal to semi-formal and the occasional tie-less gentlemen was to be seen in the dining room. Still, the hotel maintained its old traditions of elegance and popularized them as well. In the post-war years a major radio broadcasting

Princess Margaret visited the hotel on 28 July 1958.

room was installed in one of the hotel towers and for many years people across Canada could tune in nightly to the big band arrangements of Mart Kenney or Moxie Whitney: "From the spacious ballroom of the Banff Springs Hotel, situated mile-high in the Canadian Rockies..."

By the mid-1960s, the hotel was almost exclusively catering to conventions, bus tours, and automobile-oriented families. The days of the private coach on the mainline had died as surely as had the old six-horse carriage. But the old can rarely pass on without something new pushing in to fill the gap, and for each tradition being broken there is usually a new one in the process of becoming. In 1969, the hotel fulfilled the dream of earlier managements by remaining open for the winter season—Banff was finally becoming the winter resort promised 60 years before. Perhaps it was with that first winter season the hotel, complete with après-ski lounges, rock bands, and a young crowd vying for attention with all the vigour of those young ladies in their ridicule-defying outfits of 1925, reached a new position—a grand old hotel wending its way through the Age of Aquarius.

The hotel required an immense amount of work – at least one guest in that winter of 1969 ranked his accommodation on a par with his old college dorm room – and it needed someone to take up its cause. Fortunately, it found such a champion in Ivor Petrak, former CPR employee who returned to the company to become hotel manager in 1971. Petrak brought to the hotel not only a solid background in hotel management but, even more critically, a sensitivity to the Banff Springs' history and a determination to restore the hotel to its former grandeur, though in a contemporary context. "Van Horne had the vision," Petrak was fond saying, "I had the mission."

Accordingly, he went to work, not only on the hotel but on the CPR board of directors, convincing them to recommit the company to the old standards excellence. Petrak's own commitment was total. In the first year, he began reworking the hotel from top to bottom. Step one was to repaint and refurnish 75 rooms on the ninth floor. The following year, catering to winter guests, he converted the old Garden View Lounge into a warm, intimate dining club and lounge called the Rob Roy Room (now the Bow Valley Grill), and put in a new cabaret in the downstairs arcade. Thereafter, he redid 150 rooms a year – carpentry, painting, bedspreads, upholstery – drawing heavily the sensibilities and inspiration of Lazlo Funtek, a respected theatre set designer from the Banff Centre. In 1975 he rewired the hotel and elevator, a $20-million job, and three years later updated the plumbing for another $15 million. He also reworked the arcade floor a second time, creating space for a number of small shops, boutiques and restaurants, and he continued to convert unused space to guest rooms and suites.

Living With Inflation

The book you hold in front of you, *Banff Springs: The Story of a Hotel,* was first published in 1973. In the first edition, the final chapter was filled with interesting facts of the day, including this passage:

"Depending upon the season and the particular room involved, guests will pay from $18 to $30 for a single room, $24 to $38 for a double, and $55 to $110 for a suite."

Ivor Petrak shows Canadian Prime Minister Pierre Trudeau through the hotel during a 1970s visit.

One such room (now Room 457), for instance, was fashioned from a housekeeper's apartment, which in turn had been built around one of the old hotel staircases. In its interesting configuration, the room features a bedroom and sitting area separated by a gracious set of stairs, two meters (six feet) wide, that double back and sweep majestically up to the bathroom, which, to its credit, features a large jetted tub and one of just two bidets in the entire hotel.

Those renovations, however, were only Petrak's opening salvo. In the fall of 1980, having been through the hotel once to ensure the service infrastructure was modern and its accommodation "adequate," he launched a new campaign to bring all the rooms and public spaces closer to the standard he sought. This time around, the instructions were that each room receive individual attention and detailing, with no one design being repeated more than three times in the entire hotel.

The Admiral's Suite, as photographed by renowned black and white photographer Craig Richards, was one of many guest rooms Petrak had built in imaginative locations.

The outside swimming pool was also rebuilt for four seasons—in the winter, when air temperatures hover well below freezing, it becomes a welcoming, steaming hot pool for weary skiers and snowboarders. Petrak's passion for turning old corners into new rooms continued unabated. He began to enclose some exterior balconies and odd outside crannies, creating in the process unique public spaces like the Van Horne Room (now the Ivor Petrak Room), which was originally a balcony above the hotel entrance, and guest rooms like the ground floor Admiral's Suite. For

The Admiral's Suite has been removed, but this distinctive circular window remains in the wall of the William Wallace Room.

as long as anyone could remember, the attic in the north wing had been used for storage, with a few beds set up for staff. Petrak had this part of the hotel converted to a string of 8th floor guest rooms, where visitors today enjoy some of best views in the entire hotel, albeit with quirky rooflines.

By 1982, more than $60 million had gone into the hotel, and still Petrak showed no sign of slowing down. As early as 1976, Parks Canada had approved an elaborate, two-phase program that would change both the hotel and its grounds, but it wasn't until after a number of political and financial obstacles had been cleared in 1985 that the hotel was able to begin the project. Phase I, with a budget of $37.5 million, saw the conversion of the old staff building called the Annex into a new 250–room guest wing called the Manor; the construction of 336 new staff apartments (which, according to Petrak, "provide

This arched walkway links the main hotel to the Manor Wing.

the best staff accommodation in the world"), and 35 townhouses for senior staff on land just west of the hotel; and the addition of a new clubhouse and nine additional golf holes to the existing golf facilities. With the exception of the golf course improvements, the Phase I work was completed in time for the 1988 centennial celebrations.

In the hotel proper, cozy little two-floor honeymoon suites complete with spiral stairs, heart-shaped headboards and Jacuzzis were tucked into the uppermost tower turrets, and the hotel's most luxurious suite, the Presidential, was fashioned from staff quarters on the 10th floor and empty space on the 11th and 12 floors. Opened in December of 1986, the suite featured marble, brass and plush fabrics throughout, a glass elevator to transport guests from floor to floor, eight bedrooms with canopied beds and ornate original wall

An official photo of hotel manager Ivor Petrak and designer Laslo Funtek in the Presidential Suite.

An aerial view of the hotel taken in 1985. The town of Banff can be seen across the river in the background.

tapestries, a reception foyer and fireplace, private concierge service, a lap pool, and a multilevel living room with baby grand piano, loft library, stereo system and big screen television. Known today as the Presidential Tower, the spread of rooms is occasionally rented in its entirely, but is also sold as separate rooms, anchored by the Presidential Suite, which is still the best room in the house. It comes complete with a toilet wedged into a little corner of one of the bathrooms that offers those who use it a glorious unimpeded overlook of the confluence of the Bow and Spray Rivers – the old "million dollar view." Because of the awkward configuration of the turret corner in which it sits, the toilet took carpenters and plumbers nearly three days to install, but the view from its seat alone nearly justifies the price—up to $5,000 a night.

Indira Ghandi is welcomed to the hotel by Ivok Petrak.

There is no shortage of guests who can afford the Presidential Suite. With the almost continual renovations, the number of royalty, politicians and celebrities visiting the hotel through the 1970s and 80s was as high as it ever was: Prime Ministers Trudeau, Clark and Mulroney, Lord Mountbatten, Prince Philip, Princess Alexandria, the Duke and Duchess of Kent, Indira Ghandi, Prince Norihito and Princess Takamatsu of Japan, Prince Rainier, Arnold Schwarzenegger and Maria Shriver, Jack Lemmon, Lee Marvin, Margot Kidder, and Brooke Shields.

And, as in the past, the presence of celebrities added to the store of hotel anecdotes. When Prince Bernhardt of the Netherlands stayed at the hotel in October of 1972, he entered an elevator one day to be confronted by a chipper, chatty and obviously unwitting female elevator attendant. After exchanging greetings and pleasantries about the weather, the young woman smiled at the Prince and asked, "And what do you do when you're not staying with us?" "Actually," replied a bemused Prince Bernhardt, "I'm a prince." "All right!" said the young lady, extending her hand. "And I'm the Queen of England. Pleased to meet you."

Local musician Louis Trono played for hotel guests for over 70 years.

Although renovation encouraged the rich and famous to visit the hotel once again, modernization did little to dispel the notion of the hotel as a haunted castle. Elegant ghosts in formal evening dress were rumoured to make occasional appearances in the Rob Roy Room, now the Bow Valley Grill, with the wrinkle that they appear only from the waist up. The floor of the new lounge was constructed some three feet above the original and it appears the ghosts still stalk the old level. There is also a story about some guests who returned to their room one night to find the lock to their door jammed. They called down to the bell desk for help, but when the bellboy arrived, he found the party sitting comfortably in their room. They thanked him for coming up, but said they had already been assisted by an elderly man in a uniform different from that worn by the bellboys. Their description was of a deceased bell captain who had often that, given the chance, he would like to come back to hotel as a ghost once he had passed on.

DEEP END
NO DIVING

CHAPTER 9

A CENTURY OF TRADITIONS MERGE WITH MODERN TIMES

"...blending architectural and historic charm with state-of-the-art appointments and facilities."

With or without ghosts, in 1988, the year of its centennial, various styles were encountered in the hotel—ranging the breadth of Gothic and Renaissance architecture and decoration while exhibiting influences of England, France, Scotland, Switzerland and Spain—keeping alive the suggestion of an elegant and romantic past. In this regard, the hotel fulfilled the ideal of all the early Canadian Pacific Railway hotels as imagined by Van Horne and Price. In recognition of this achievement, on March 22, 1988, 100 years since welcoming its first guests, the Banff Springs Hotel was declared a National Historical Site by the Sites and Monuments Board of Canada.

This recognition coincided with a surge of brisk business, but the Banff Springs and its sister railway hotels across the country were once again in need of a major injection of capital. Around $100 million was budgeted to return the hotel to its former glory, while also adapting to changing needs of the vacation and convention market and modernizing the structure with the addition of air-conditioning, electronic door keys, and in-room Internet access.

The Conference Centre (left foreground) was designed to blend seamlessly with the main hotel.

The Banff Springs Hotel had always hosted large functions, but the addition of a dedicated conference centre in 1990 added greatly to the capacity. Designed by Carruthers, Marshall, and Associates, the curved structure backs onto the lower slopes of Sulphur Mountain and faces a bronze casting of William Cornelius Van Horne in the centre of a flower-filled traffic circle. (Throughout the hotel, small bronze plaques depict Van Horne pointing in the direction of the convention centre). Blending perfectly with the style of the main hotel building, the convention centre features a Rundlestone façade, a gabled roofline, and replica period furnishings. The 13,940-square-meter (150,000-square-foot) layout includes four large function rooms, 10 smaller meeting rooms, a 250-seat theatre, a conservatory, an area for outdoor gatherings, and a small number of guest rooms perfectly situated for event organizers. With rear access large enough to drive vehicles onto the main floor, high ceilings, and huge chandeliers that can be removed when required, it also allows

A Castle in My Backyard

Living in the mountains you always know where you are. There is always a mountain I know looking at me; the Bow River is at my side or I can see the Banff Springs Hotel, which has been a landmark to me for over seventy years. All demand equal recognition.

I was nine years old when I first got lost in the Banff Springs Hotel. Mind you, it was planned. Growing up in Banff in the depression years of the 1930s we had to make up games, and getting lost in the hotel was one of them. To us it was a magic castle. We didn't have the powers of Harry Potter, but if we had, that is where we would have practiced our wizardry.

They were exciting years. The cliental looked like they stepped from the pages of the Great Gadsby or the screen of a current movie, as many did. The Prince of Wales honoured the hotel with visits and a trophy for golf competition. The beauty and mystique continued as Hollywood stars, Ginger Rogers, Bing Crosby, Mickey Rooney and others came to play.

The hotel gave me an introduction to earning money–first as a caddie on the golf course and later as a Brewster agent in the hotel. I could be called a pioneer in this area as I made some of the earliest air reservations for holiday travelers, just after World War II.

The Banff Springs Hotel may not be officially listed as a castle, but to many of us who grew up in it's shadow, it is, and more.

–Eddie Hunter, Banff resident since 1934

the hotel to host a great variety of events. The largest meeting room is the 1,400-square-meter (15,000-square-foot) Van Horne Ballroom, which can hold 1,000 guests for dinner. Like the Van Horne, the other function rooms are named for past presidents of the Canadian Pacific Railway. When delegates fill the centre, the real action takes place behind the scenes, where staff in a cavernous "finishing kitchen," complete with a conveyor belt to help get food properly presented in a timely manner, add final touches to meals that have been partially prepared in the hotel's main kitchens.

At street level of the Conference Centre, facing out to the traffic circle, the design incorporated retail space. Unlike the boutiques and speciality shops found in the Lobby Level arcade, Conference Centre tenants mostly provide practical services to visitors and staff—a grocery store, a liquor store, a business centre with public Internet access, car rentals, and a sports clothing and rental outlet. The exception is Gallery at the Springs, selling a wide range of souvenirs, and the Bowling Centre, with four lanes of indoor five-pin bowling.

"The development of a substantial health spa facility at the Banff Springs Hotel is an appropriate intervention in keeping with the hotel's reputation as a leading Canadian example of a large-scale resort hotel."

– Parks Canada review of proposed health spa, 1994

Meanwhile, architect Robert LeBlond and interior designer Kerry Busby were commissioned for renovations to the hotel itself. Coinciding with this period of change, in 1990, Ted Kissane was appointed the new general manager of the Banff Springs Hotel. After the sudden death of Ivor Petrak in 1991, Kissane took on the

An artist's rendering of the new spa facility, 1994.

expanded role of managing the other mountain properties owned by the railway company.

In 1995, the Solace Spa opened. Spa services had been a tradition since the hotel first opened, but the Solace was different. This was an upscale amenity along the lines of classic European spas, yet was integrated fully with the rest of the hotel. Beyond the heavy glass doors separating the spa from busy hotel hallways is an oasis of peace—a place where it is possible for complete relaxation. The 3,250-square-metre (35,000-square-foot) facility is anchored by a magnificent Romanesque mineral pool, whose mosaic of blue and green tiles create an almost surreal ambience. An underwater speaker sound system and mood lighting add to the appeal. Off to one side is a series of three waterfalls, each a different temperature, that fill three private pools. Large windows provide a view to outdoor whirlpools, which are especially popular on snowy winter days. Complete with his and her sitting areas bedecked with fresh fruit, hot drinks, and daily newspapers, even the changing room facilities are memorably luxurious. Other services on offer include massage therapies, aromatherapy, body treatments, facials, hair services, and more.

The centrepiece of the Willow Stream is this magnificent mineral pool.

Back in 1986 two wings, which had been serving as staff accommodation since 1926, were converted to guest rooms. Busby set about bringing rooms in the two wings up to the same high standard as the rest of the hotel. Unveiled in 1997, the Manor-Highland Wing reopened with a traditional Scottish look throughout guest rooms and public areas. During this same revamp, the Tudor House décor was designed to reflect the traditions of an English country estate, with a cream, ivy, and rose colour theme and dark, solid furnishings, but it has since been refurnished to better blend with the style of the rest of the hotel. Today, the two wings come together in a quiet lobby where a portrait of Queen Alexandra (1844-1925) looks down on guests relaxing in comfortable seating set around two fireplaces.

This turret above the Willow Stream fits perfectly with the style of the hotel.

In 2001, the hotel, along with other CPR hotels, was re-branded. Its official name was now the Fairmont Banff Springs. The following year, the the Solace Spa was renamed Willow Stream, in line with the brand name adopted for spa facilities at other Fairmont properties.

For visitors who are returning to the hotel after a decade or more, the most obvious change is the magnificent lobby facing Spray Avenue, which opened in 2001. The original exterior façade of the centre tower now creates a rugged, almost

The most recent hotel renovation included the construction of a new guest entrance on the west side of the main building.

Medieval feel to the interior of the new lobby, which has been extended out to a new entry way for visitors checking into the hotel. The cavernous lobby is filled with dominant features such as Rundlestone columns, a high vaulted ceiling, and two massive stone stairways leading up into the heart of the hotel. In keeping with tradition, the flooring is Tyndall limestone, covered in sections by handcrafted carpet with the embroidered words *Semper Eadem* (Always the Same), a Latin motto that appears on the stained glass windows of the Mount Stephen Hall. Medieval chandeliers, hand-carved wooden chairs, heavy drapes, and period lighting add to the appeal of the place where most guests first experience the hotel.

Heritage Hall, a changing display of historic photos related to the hotel, provides an

The gracious style of the new lobby mirrors the rest of the hotel.

Once bustling with arriving and departing guests, the original lobby is now Rundle Hall, a peaceful public space.

interesting diversion directly above the lobby, while across the hallway from Heritage Hall, the Banffshire Club provides the most dignified dining experience in all of Banff.

On the east side of the hotel, the original lobby is now a beautifully historic and peaceful space renamed Rundle Hall. Windows frame spectacular views of the Bow River and Mount Rundle while off to one side is the William Wallace Room, a public space complete with a log fireplace and comfortable couches. The courtyard entrance, leading into Rundle Hall from the traffic circle, is now used to receive dignitaries and for special occasions. At the top of the grand stairway leading up to the Rundle Lounge is the hotel's largest painting. Measuring over six square metres (67 square feet), it features forestry workers in New Brunswick cutting masts for the British navy.

After 15 years running the hotel, and with the renovations complete, Ted Kissane retired as general manager in 2005. His position was taken by a new Regional Vice President and General Manager, David Roberts, who arrived in Banff via Hawaii. Roberts' role also includes overseeing operations of Fairmont properties in Lake Louise, Jasper, and Calgary. Born and raised in Kenya, then educated in England, Roberts has previous been employed at London's Dorchester Hotel and at hotel properties in the U.S. Virgin Islands and Hawaii.

Today, driving up to the hotel from downtown Banff, Spray Avenue ends at a traffic circle. In the centre of the traffic circle, surrounded by flowers in summer, is a bronze statue of William Cornelius Van Horne. Although he overlooks a creation that might now impress him in the way the original hotel surprised old Morley Roberts, there is little doubt Van Horne would recognize it with approval—a sumptuous castle in the wilderness, welcoming in style travelers from all over the world.

William Van Horne seems to be directing vehicles from the hotel's traffic circle.

Chapter 10

The Banff Springs Today

"...laurels alone cannot keep the beds made or the wine cellar full."

As the hotel moves through its second century, it finds itself somewhat in the position of the grand old men of the mountains—it can settle back a bit, its reputation established, and recall the good old days of the unblemished wilderness experience. But, unlike the grand old men, the hotel does not know just how old it is; for while it remembers a long and multi-hued past, its future may well span a period of time which would make its years to date seem short.

As a non-retiring institution then, the hotel lives

on from day-to-day—its laurels alone cannot keep the beds made or the wine cellar full. Although most guests of the hotel are unaware of either the cost or complexity involved in keeping the systems running smoothly, anyone who spends more than a few days in the building finds his curiosity piqued by the day-to-day business of the hotel's management.

The hotel, as anyone who has visited the place will attest, is a large building. It takes large numbers of people and large amounts of capital to maintain large buildings—especially if the building's business is to handle other large numbers of people. In 1930, after the major construction had been completed, it was estimated that the CPR had spent some $9 million on the hotel's physical structure since 1887. But that amount doesn't seem like much when compared to what it would cost to reconstruct the building from scratch today—if someone could be found who would be capable of handling the work.

Much of the daily overhead goes toward paying the salaries of the hotel staff, which, in the peak months of July and August, numbers 1,000-1,150. A rough breakdown of that figure shows 400 persons involved with housekeeping, 500 in food and beverage, close to 60 in administration. Other services—grounds, maintenance, valet, and recreation—account for the remaining staff.

Through most of its life, the Banff Springs Hotel had opened only during the warmer months of the year. As a result, the vast majority of its staff were students working through their summer break. The staffing mentality remained the same beyond

Banff Springs Hotel Viewpoints

Golfers enjoy one of the most famous hotel vistas as they approach the 14th green of the Banff Springs Golf Course. Here are a few other places that offer different hotel perspectives:

Surprise Corner: From the end of Buffalo Street, walk across the road from the parking lot to a flight of stairs that lead to a log-sided lookout with uninterrupted hotel views. Interpretive boards describe the scene.

The hotel from Surprise Corner

Sulphur Mountain: The Banff Gondola transports visitors from beside the Upper Hot Springs to the summit of this peak on the edge of town. Looking down from the summit, it becomes obvious how small the hotel is compared to the surrounding wilderness.

Tunnel Mountain: There's no gondola to the summit of this peak, but it's easily reached on foot in 40 minutes from St. Julien Road. The hotel comes into full view just below the summit, and from the fenced lookouts at the back of the mountain, the golf course can be seen laid out in all its glory.

Mount Norquay: Drive up the Mount Norquay Road and stop at the last switchback. Here, at a place known locally as the "bald spot" (looking up form town you will see why), the Banff Springs rises majestically between Rundle and Sulphur Mountains.

1969, when the hotel began opening year-round. But as a result of new recruiting methods and improved employee relations, the level of service improved greatly, while at the same time employee turnover was drastically reduced. Currently at least four employees, including executive chef Martin Luthi, have worked at the hotel for more than 30 years. The longest serving employee is Dave Moberg, Guest Relations Manager, who has been employed at the hotel since 1962.

The number of hotel guests is nearly as impressive as the number of staff. The record number of guests which the hotel has hosted at one time is well over 1,000, but this figure doesn't take into consideration the fact that the hotel operates at close-to-capacity volume throughout the summer season. And since most of the guests are short-stay visitors, the hotel will experience a complete visitor turnover up to three times a week.

Fairmont Room.

There are 778 guest rooms, down from a high of 850 rooms before the most recent round of renovations. Rooms are laid out in nine configurations, with the least expensive Fairmont Room providing anything but standard accommodations. There are four different suite styles, including the 92-square-meter (1,000-square-foot) Presidential Suite.

Junior Suite.

In the field of recreation, the hotel today carries on the traditions of the past while expanding the list of available activities to include a few peculiar to the late twentieth century. In addition to the Willow Stream spa facility, the hotel features indoor and outdoor heated pools, tennis courts, five-pin bowling, its own corral and trail riding operation, and a 27-hole golf course. Through the hotel, guests can book fly-fishing trips along the Bow River, boat tours on Lake Minnewanka, and general sightseeing tours. Winter guests mostly spend their days skiing or snowboarding at three nearby resorts, but the cooler months also see the creation of an ice skating rink below the hotel. Guests can also try tobogganing and cross-country skiing, or have the concierge book sleigh rides or dog-sledding.

Operations dealing with food offer another interesting insight into the complexity of the

Hotel Dining

Whether guests or not, most visitors to Banff drop by to see one of the town's biggest tourist attractions, and a meal here might not be as expensive as you think. The hotel itself has more eateries than most small towns–from a deli serving soup and snacks to the finest of fine dining.

The Banffshire Club provides the finest of fine dining.

Banffshire Club: Seating just 76 diners, this is the hotel's most formal dining room.

Bow Valley Grill: Impressive buffets are the main draw at this cavernous dining room. Sunday brunch is legendary.

Castello Ristorante: Ensconced in an octagonal room of the Manor Wing, this seductive dining room has a menu dominated by Italian favourites.

Castle Pantry: Open 24 hours daily, this casual café is at the north end of the lobby.

Golf Course Clubhouse: A seasonal restaurant with a wrap-around deck offering sweeping mountain views.

Grapes: An intimate yet casual wine bar noted for its fine cheeses and fondues.

Ramsey Lounge: This elegant lounge in the Manor Wing is the perfect place for a quiet drink.

Rundle Lounge: A long, narrow piano bar, where many tables offer views down the Bow Valley.

Samurai Restaurant: A small yet traditional Japanese restaurant near the entrance to the Willow Stream spa.

Waldhaus: Originally a clubhouse for the golf course, the building now holds a downstairs bar and an upstairs dining room where German specialities dominate the menu.

hotel's management. Swiss-born Martin Luthi was first employed at the hotel in 1974 and has been Executive Chef since 1980. "I have an undying passion for food, cooking and my job here at the Banff Springs Hotel," enthuses Luthi. "I am continually motivated by the beauty of the Canadian Rockies and strive to translate that into the art of cuisine." His responsibility is no small one, for there are 12 kitchens that handle 1.2 million meals annually. The kitchens are staffed by up to 150 trained chefs, some whose specialty is desserts, of which 500,000 are created annually. In addition to preparing meals for 10 restaurants, around 300,000 meals are whisked through the hotel to guest rooms as room service. As you may expect, the most popular meat is Alberta beef, including well over two tons of striploin, the most popular cut, ordered annually. Over 30,000 litres (7,900 gallons) of milk are consumed each year, and the amount of premium bacon used weighs in at nearly 1,800 kilograms (4,000 pounds). During this same period of time, there are some 100,000 eggs eaten, and nearly 15,000 loafs of bread disappear from the hotel's tables.

Much of the food stores come from one supplier, Bridgebrand, while specialty items may be shipped in seasonally from suppliers as far away as Ontario. The hotel will fly in over 1,000 pounds of salmon a month during the summer season, much of it used in Chef Luthi's signature dish—salmon marinated in whisky and baked on a cedar plank.

What are the eaters of all this Alberta beef doing at the hotel? Much of the business in the last three decades has come from two sources—tours and conventions, with independent travelers, private functions such as weddings, and academic conferences rounding out the typical hotel guest.

The hotel does not, contrary to the notion of many guests, sit back passively and wait for business to come its way. Although many of the tours and conventions represent "repeat" business coming from firms and companies which have dealt with the hotel in the past, the Banff Springs management actively seeks out new business as it encourages business of the past to visit again. The hotel will also sell itself on a corporate basis. Representatives, say, from four or five Fairmont hotels will make a trip to the United States to visit various executives and travel agents in that country and invite them to visit the hotels and see for themselves what the different institutions have to offer in the way of tourist and convention facilities.

The hotel deals with over 50 different touring companies, most of which run a continuing series of trips through the Rockies throughout the summer months. Most tours spend one or two nights at the hotel, operating on the modified American plan of room and two meals a day. During the winter months special chartered "ski-week" packages help to bolster the hotel's business.

Just as tours are big business in summer and winter, conventions are big business in spring and fall. In the course of any given year the hotel will host up to 300 conventions and functions. In addition to a fulltime staff of 12 who plan and organize conventions, the hotel employs a dedicated group sales team, who work independently from the tour and leisure sales teams. The hotel also employs 35 banquet staff. For large events,

Fairmont Monte Carlo

Corporate Shuffling

In 1988, the Canadian Pacific Railway purchased hotels owned by Canadian National, including the Jasper Park Lodge, and formed a new company, Canadian Pacific Hotels and Resorts (CP Hotels). A decade later, CP Hotels purchased Delta Hotels, an upscale chain that had grown from humble Vancouver beginnings to be represented in most major Canadian cities. In 1999, CP Hotels added the U.S.-based Fairmont hotel chain to its portfolio and in 2001 re-branded itself as Fairmont Hotels and Resorts.

In 2006, with Fairmont positioned as North America's largest luxury hotel chain, the company was acquired by Colony Capital and Kingdom Hotels International. In addition to historically significant hotels and resorts across Canada, the company manages upscale properties across the United States, including Fairmont Franz Klammer Lodge (Telluride, Colorado), Fairmont Orchid (Hawaii), and Fairmont Scottsdale Princess (Scottsdale, Arizona). Further afield, you can stay in Fairmont properties in Mexico, Bermuda, Barbados, London, Scotland, Monaco, Kenya, and the United Arab Emirates.

Rising majestically from the surrounding forest, the Banff Springs is as much a landmark today as it was a century ago.

a roster of trained, part-time staff who work other jobs in town are called up to the hotel.

Most events one-off affairs, but some are annual events that the hotel and indeed the town of Banff have come to embrace. The longest running of these is the Oilmen's Convention, hosted by the hotel in odd-numbered years and by the Jasper Park Lodge in even-numbered years. What began in 1951 as a small golf tournament has grown into a five-day extravaganza of socializing between oil executives from around the world, complete with professional golfers such as Fuzzy Zoeller giving instruction clinics and entertainment provided by top-notch singers.

Hollywood celebrities fill the hotel each January for the Fairmont Banff Springs Celebrity Sports Invitational, which combines ski racing at Sunshine Village with hotel events designed to raise money for the Waterkeeper Alliance, an environmental organization led by Robert F. Kennedy. Unlike most conventions, this one includes a grand public dinner in the Van Horne Ballroom.

Some conventions are memorable even for those not affiliated with the hotel. In 2006, over 800 delegates from the Texas Roadhouse restaurant chain booked out the hotel for their annual conference. After ensuring the hotel's statue of William Van Horne was suitably donned in a cowboy hat, the company put on a parade down Banff's main street, filled the local food bank with donated items, and spruced up the local senior's centre with a coat of paint, while also helping Hurricane Katrina victims by building a dozen homes in Banff's Central Park that were shipped by truck to New Orleans.

CHAPTER 11

BANFF SPRINGS GOLF COURSE

"...the most expensive ever built, having cost over half a million dollars."

Gazing out from the hotel's Bow Valley Terrace, it is impossible not to be impressed by the setting of the Banff Springs Golf Course, with its location beside the glacial-blue Bow River and surrounded by snowcapped mountains. The terrace panorama is just a taste of what golfers experience down on the course, beginning with the picturesque drive past turbulent Bow Falls and over the sparkling Spray River onto the course proper. Regarded as one of the world's most scenic golf courses, the layout is also renowned for a long and storied history, the iconic Devil's Cauldron hole, and an abundance of wildlife.

The hotel's first course, just nine holes, was laid out in 1911 by Scotsman William Thomson. Filling part of an alluvial plain known as the Bow Flats, with the Bow River coming into play on many holes and the hotel visible in the distance, hole lengths ranged from 160 to 500 yards. Fairways were defined by keeping natural grasses cut low and sand from the riverbank was spread across tightly cut "greens." The original clubhouse, a simple affair facing the first tee, has since been converted to the superintendent's residence. It is passed on the cart path between the 12th green and 13th tee. In that first summer season of 1911, green fees were 50 cents per round or $1 per day.

In 1917, management of the course was turned over to the government, with the understanding the course would be expanded to 18 holes. In 1919, the government employed famed golf architect Donald Ross to advise on the expanded layout, but it wasn't until 1924 that the redesigned course officially opened. Three years later, the Canadian Pacific Railway regained control of the course. Around the same time, the Canadian National had employed Stanley Thompson to design a course for their Jasper hotel. Having opened to rave reviews, the CPR brought Thompson in to design a new layout for Banff. Money was no barrier for the wealthy railway company and when unveiled in 1928, the new Banff Springs Golf Course was the most expensive ever built, having cost over half a million dollars. Topsoil for the fairways was brought in from the prairies and sand for Thompson's generous bunkers from British Columbia. The new layout incorporated some of Ross's holes, but also some stunning new ones. None was more iconic than the 8th, over a small glacial lake nestled below the impossibly steep face of Mount Rundle. Now played as the 4th and known as the Devil's

Stanley Thompson

Regarded by golf historians as one of the world's preeminent course architects, Stanley Thompson is little known outside of Canada. Born in Toronto in 1893, Thompson and his four brothers were all accomplished golfers, winning many national titles between them in the 1920s. But it was in designing courses rather than playing them that Stanley Thompson found fame. His designs were significant for their use of natural features, a throwback to links courses of Scotland. Irregular bunkers on direct lines between tee and green and holes aligned with distant mountains are also classic Thompson traits.

In addition to the Banff Springs Golf Course, he designed famous layouts such as Jasper Park Lodge Golf Course, Highland Links (Nova Scotia), and St. George's Golf and Country Club (Ontario), along with over 140 other courses in Canada and the United States. Many of his best-known courses are public links, with reasonable fees and easy access to all.

Later in life, Thompson became known as much for his golf course design as his flamboyant attire, his love of whisky, and his colourful stories. Robert Trent Jones Snr. was employed by Thompson's design company and with Donald Ross, the three men were charter members of the American Society of Golf Course Architects.

Thompson died in 1953, penniless after losing multiple fortunes. To those he owed money, his debts were forgiven for the joy he had given them all over the years, or so the story goes.

Cauldron, it is one of the most famously scenic holes in the world of golf. Thompson's design also incorporated the area between the hotel and the clubhouse (which had formerly been used as a campground), with the elevated tee box for the new first hole being directly below the hotel and requiring an admirable hit over the Spray River to a wide fairway far below. The redesigned course was 6,625 yards from the back markers and played to a par of 73. A solid Tudor-style stone clubhouse—with a dining room, patio, locker rooms, and pro-shop—was constructed next to the first tee. The ceremonial opening shot was hit from the new first tee on 1 August 1928 by the pioneering outfitter Tom Wilson. Immediately, the Canadian Pacific Railway began promoting the course as a highlight of Banff, with guests encouraged to stay at the Banff Springs Hotel of course.

Tom Wilson teeing off at the official opening of the Banff Springs Golf Course.

Radio actor Tommy Tweed donned a suit of in armour for this 1930s promotional shot of the Banff Springs Golf Course.

By the 1960s, park visitation had increased dramatically and with it the need for more facilities. A second golf course was proposed near Johnson Lake, but never built. By the 1980s, course usage was at an all time high, the driving range needed lengthening, the clubhouse needed expanding, and parking was a major problem. Ivor Petrak, general manager of the hotel, came forward with a radical proposal that was eventually accepted—to build a much larger clubhouse and add an additional nine holes in the centre of the course. To have golfers start and finish at the new clubhouse required a change in hole numbering from (but not the order of) Thompson's layout. The original 1st hole is now the 15th, the 8th (Devil's Cauldron) is now the 4th, and the memorable walk toward the hotel on what was originally the 18th hole is now done on the 14th. (The original ordering is hinted at on the scorecard, where hole names have remained the same, including "Jinx," originally the 13th hole and now the 9th). With sweeping views across the golf course and mountains, the new clubhouse opened in 1989. Mimicking a native tepee, it is hexagonal in shape, with large windows and a wrap-around deck making the most of the surrounding mountain scenery. The old stone clubhouse, immediately below the hotel, was converted to the Waldhaus Restaurant.

Long-time professional Malcolm Tapp teaching Marilyn Monroe the finer points of golf at the Devil's Cauldron in 1953.

Over the years, many minor changes had been made to Stanley Thompson's design, and the turf had suffered heavily through snow-covered winters and heavy summer traffic. In the late 1990s, the entire course was rebuilt, using photographs from Thompson's era, the introduction of historic grasses, and new tee boxes to keep Thompson's hazards in play for modern, long-hitting golfers. In tandem with the completion of the restoration in 1999, the course gained accreditation from the Audubon Cooperative Sanctuary Program.

Viewing wildlife on the Banff Springs Golf Course is a great thrill, but the animals can also be a hazard. In 1925, elk were introduced to Banff National Park and took an immediate liking to the open fairways of the golf course and its imported grass. These large mammals have remained present ever since and, for a time, the course was fenced to keep them off the greens at night. Living on the course year-round, they are most active during the rutting season (September and October), when bull elk gather their harems and piercing calls can be heard beyond the course boundaries. Other wildlife present includes black and grizzly bears, deer, coyotes, and Canadian geese. Cougars and moose are infrequent visitors, but occasionally spotted by golfers.

Over the last 90 years, the fairways of the Banff Springs Golf Course have played host to celebrities, royalty, and famous golfers. Prince of Wales (the future King Edward VIII), was so taken with the area he donated the Prince of Wales Cup for a competition that let the winner to be in possession of the cup over winter. Gene Sarazen, one of the few golfers ever to win the "Grand Slam" of majors, played an exhibition match at Banff in 1936, and Bobby Locke did the same in 1948. In the fall of 1961, *Shell's Wonderful World of Golf* was filmed at the course, with the match featuring Stan Leonard, one of Canada's most successful golfers, competing against two-time major winner Jackie Burke Junior. In 2006, the Banff Springs Golf Course hosted some of the sport's most famous names when Jack Nicklaus, Greg Norman, Stephen Ames, John Daly, and Sergio Garcia teed it up for the Telus Skins, an annual event in Canada since

> *"Marry me, Sergio. You can still play golf."*
>
> – female fan to Sergio Garcia during the 2006 Telus Skins

Five of the world's most recognisable golfers competed at the Banff Springs Golf Course at the Telus Skins in 2006.

1993. The crowd roared with wild abandon when larger-than-life John Daly sunk the winning putt on the 17th hole, but the sentimental favourite was Jack Nicklaus, whose presence alone proved a memorable experience for all in attendance.

Although the course itself is open to public play, membership of the Banff Springs Golf Club is restricted to town residents. The club was originally formed in 1911, coinciding with the opening of the first course. In 1928, the club secured playing privileges for its members on a course that to this day is company-owned but on land leased from the government. Today, membership is limited to 200 adults and 75 juniors. As has been the case since the 1920s, nominated residents of Banff can only be elected to the club by unanimous vote at a secret ballot. Club competitions are held throughout the summer season, with ladies playing Tuesday afternoons and the men on Wednesday. Since Hugh Gourlay was crowned first club champion in 1923, members have competed in many traditional annual events. In addition to being one of the few clubs in North America where the club champion is decided by match play, many annual events have long and storied histories. The Captain's Pin dates to 1923, the season-ending Tombstone Tournament to 1925, and the family-run Gourlay scotch fourball was first contested in 1947. The Thompson Shield is a matchplay event pitting members against hotel staff and the Bray/McCullough is named for prominent past members. Women members have been competing for the Jim Brewster Challenge Cup since 1919.

William Thomson, who had laid out the original nine holes in 1911, retired as club professional in 1949. Thomson was replaced by Malcolm Tapp, at the time a promising young golfer from British Columbia, who retired forty years later in 1988. After having just two head professionals in 77 years, the position was filled by Calgarian Doug Wood, who had previous been employed at the Canmore Golf Club and was later employed as the hotel's director of golf. The head teaching pro is long-time Banff resident Scott Holland, who does an admirable job teaching younger members of the Banff Springs Golf Club the finer points of the game, but is also known for his inclusion in the *Guinness Book of Records* for playing 221 holes of golf in under 12 hours.

The Banff Springs Golf Course is a "resort course" in that it is affiliated with a hotel, but it also open to the general public, with green fee players making up the bulk of golfers through a season that usually runs from early May to early October. This means that anyone can tee it up at one of the world's most famous courses.

Heritage Hall, above the lobby, showcases the hotel's history.

Appendix

Many present-day visitors to the Banff Springs Hotel find the general decor and furnishing of the building provide a rich and exciting area for investigation. Compiled here are some data that might help answer the questions of such interested guests.

Architectural Periods

Mount Stephen Hall. The Mount Stephen Hall is one of the great halls of the North American continent. It is representative of 15th century Gothic architecture and was named for Lord Mount Stephen, first President of the CPR. Notable features include the floor of Bedford lime flagstones, the stained-glass crests in the windows (see Crests, below), and the great oak ceiling beams which feature crests of the Provinces of Alberta, British Columbia, Manitoba, New Brunswick, Nova Scotia, Ontario, Prince Edward Island, Quebec, and Saskatchewan. Newfoundland was not a province at the time the hall was built.

Oak Room. The Oak Room, which adjoins Mount Stephen Hall, also evidences Gothic influence and is noted for its panelled walls and linenfold carvings.

Strathcona and Angus Rooms. Both the Strathcona and Angus Rooms, private dining rooms just off the Alhambra Room, are in the Norman Gothic style. The Strathcona Room has a balcony that opens to the Mount Stephen Hall.

Alhambra Room. Originally a formal dining room, the Alhambra Room shows strong Spanish Renaissance influence. Particularly notable are the cast bronze doors that guard the entrance to the room and the plaque of the Santa Maria above the fireplace in the foyer. The circular staircase that leads off the foyer offers a good example of the fossiliferous Tyndall limestone. The ceiling to the stairway exhibits some beautiful "mushroom" plasterwork, while the stairway itself is lighted by irreplaceable Tiffany lamps.

Grapes Wine Bar was named for the grape vines adorning the crown moulding.

Crests

Speculation often runs high concerning the crests and mottoes found in the Mount Stephen Hall and the Oak Room. Below is a compilation of the mottoes, their translation, and the CPR officials to whom they belonged:

Mount Stephen Hall

Contra Audentior, In Opposition More Daring, Lord Mount Stephen
Modestia et Fidelitas, Modest and Loyal, Sir Edward Beatty
A Mari Usque Ad Mare, From Sea to Sea, Dominion of Canada
Manu Forti, With a Strong Hand, Lord Thomas Shaughnessy
Nil Desperandum, Never Despairing, Sir William Van Horne
Semper Eadem, Always the Same, J. M. R. Fairbairn
Solus Christus Mea Rupes, Christ Alone is my Rock, J. W. Orrock
Omnia Vincit Amor, Love Conquers All Things, Miss Kate Treleaven
A Cuspide Corona, From the Spear a Crown, M. P. Delahanty

"Semper Eadem" translates to "Always the Same."

Oak Room

Callide Et Honeste, With Skill and Honour, W. Wainright
Fidem Servo, I Keep Faith, E. Alexander
Ne Vele Veles, Form No Vile Wish, C. E. E. Ussher
Fortitudine, With Fortitude, A. Allerton
Serviendo Guberno, I Govern by Serving, J. J. Scully
Nec Temere, Nec Timide, Neither Rashly nor Timidly, W. M. Neal

Bibliography

Books

Countess of Aberdeen. *Through Canada with a Kodak.* Edinburgh: W. H. White and Co. 1892.

Baedeker, Karl. *The Dominion of Canada: Handbook for Travellers.* New York: Charles Scribner's Sons. 1907.

Bell, Archie. *Sunset Canada.* Boston: Colonial Press, 1918.

Campbell, Robert. *I Would do it Again.* Toronto: Ryerson Press, 1959.

Dewar, Thomas R. *A Ramble Round the Globe.* London: Chatto and Windus, 1894.

Fear, G. M. *Banff and Its Beauties.* Toronto: MacFarlane. (before 1900.)

Fraser, John Foster. *Canada As It Is.* London: Cassell and Company, 1905.

Gibbon, John Murray. *Steel of Empire: The Romantic History of the Canadian Pacific.* Toronto: McClelland & Stewart, 1935.

Gowans, Alan. *Building Canada: An Architectural History of Canadian Life.* Toronto: Oxford University Press, 1966.

Hart, E.J. *Golf on the Roof of the World.* Banff: EJH Literary Enterprises, 1999.

Ingersoll, Ernest. *The Canadian Guidebook* (Part II). London: William Heinemann, 1892.

Kalman H. D. *The Railway Hotels and the Development of the Chateau Style in Canada.*

Luxton, N. K. *Fifty Switzerlands in One: Banff the Beautiful, Canada's National Park.* Banff, Luxton, 1923.

McEvoy, Bernard. *From the Great Lakes to the Wide West.* Toronto: William Briggs, 1902.

Morton, W. L., ed. *The Shield of Achilles.*
Toronto: McClelland and Stewart Limited, 1968.
(Particularly, Alan Gowans, "The Canadian National Style.")

Niven, Frederick, and W. J. Phillips. *Colour in the Canadian Rockies.*
Toronto: Thomas Nelson and Sons, Ltd., 1937.

Roberts, Morley. *On the Old Trail.*
London: Eveleigh Nash and Grayson, Ltd., 1927.

Sladen, Douglas. *On the Cars and Off.*
London: Ward, Lock, and Bowden, Ltd., 1895.

Somerset, Susan M. *Impressions of a Tenderfoot.*
London: John Murray, 1896.

Vaugh, Walter. *The Life and Work of Sir William Van Horne.*
New York: The Century Company, 1920.

Ward, Mrs. Humphrey. *Lady Merton, Colonist.*
Toronto: The Musson Book Company, 1910.

Wilcox, Walter. *Camping in the Canadian Rockies.*
New York: G. P. Putnam and Sons, 1897.

Historic Articles, Periodicals, Pamphlets

Alberta Farmer, 1926.

Annual Reports of the Department of the Interior, 1902-1921.

The Architectural Record, June 1889. Great American Architects
Series No. 5. A Review of the Works of Bruce Price.

Building, VI. February 26, 1887.

Calgary News Telegram, 1912-13.

Canadian Pacific Railway.
Banff Springs Hotel: In the Heart of the Canadian Rockies.

Crag and Canyon, Banff, 1903-2007.

Dominion Illustrated, Vols. I, IV, 1888, 1890.

Edmonton Journal, 1972.

Rogatnik, Abraham. "Canadian Castles: Phenomena of the Railway Hotel," *Architectural Reviezu*, CXLI (May, 1967).

Winnipeg Sun, 1887.

Brochure

Your Key to the Castle.
Free brochure available from the hotel concierge.

Unpublished Materials

Alice Fulmer. *The Old and a Touch of the New.*
Whyte Museum of the Canadian Rockies, Banff.

Mrs. W. S. Painter. Tape interview.
Whyte Museum of the Canadian Rockies, Banff.

Walter Painter. *Hotel floor plans.*
Whyte Museum of the Canadian Rockies, Banff.

Dorothy Whyte. Personal correspondence.

Websites

Banff Heritage Tourism: www.banffheritagetourism.com

Canadian Pacific Railway: www.cpr.ca

Canadian Pacific Railway Archives: www.cprheritage.com

Fairmont Hotels and Resorts: www.fairmont.com

Skyline Hikers of the Canadian Rockies: www.skylinehikers.ca

Stanley Thompson Society: www.stanleythompson.com

Town of Banff: www.banff.ca

Trail Riders of the Canadian Rockies: www.trail-rides.ca.

Whyte Museum of the Canadian Rockies: www.whyte.org

Index

Photography Credits

Summerthought Publishing would like to thank Fairmont Hotels & Resorts for their assistance and kind permission to photograph at the Fairmont Banff Springs. The publisher would also like to thank the following individuals, companies, and archives for permission to reproduce their work.

Title Page:

Whyte Museum of the Canadian Rockies (Byron Harmon), V263-NA3738.

Introduction:

Page 1: Bruno Engler; Page 2: Whyte Museum of the Canadian Rockies (George Noble), V92-NG3-1; Page 3: CPR Archives (R.H. Palenske), BR336.

Chapter 1:

Page 4: Whyte Museum of the Canadian Rockies, V633-NA66-1796; Page 7: Whyte Museum of the Canadian Rockies, NA66-952; Page 9: Whyte Museum of the Canadian Rockies (D. Clark), repository number unknown; Page 10: Glenbow Museum (Boorne and May), NA-2977-1; Page 12: Glenbow Museum, NA-2788-79; Page 15 (top): *Empire of Steel;* Page 15 (bottom): Cornell University Library; Page 17: Glenbow Museum (W. Notman and Son), NA-1075-4; Page 18: Glenbow Museum *(Illustrated London News),* NA-1406-245; Page 21: Glenbow Museum (Boorne and May), NA-2977-48.

Chapter 2

Page 22: Glenbow Museum, NA-637-15; Page 24: Glenbow Museum, NA-529-20; Page 27: Whyte Museum of the Canadian Rockies, V484-NA66-345; Page 28: Glenbow Museum, NA-2968-

68; Page 31: Whyte Museum of the Canadian Rockies (Walter D. Wilcox), NA66-543; Page 32: Whyte Museum of the Canadian Rockies (George Paris), V484-NA66-2018; Page 34: Whyte Museum of the Canadian Rockies, V85-NA66-577; Page 37: CPR Archives, NS.1728; Page 38: Provincial Archives of Alberta (Ernest Brown); Page 43: Whyte Museum of the Canadian Rockies (Sam Ward), NA66-2584.

Chapter 3

Page 44: CPR Archives, A.32207; Page 48, 49: Andrew Hempstead; Page 50: Whyte Museum of the Canadian Rockies, NA33-1885; Page 53: Glenbow Museum, NA-2126-19.

Chapter 4

Page 56: Glenbow Museum, NA-3267-53; Page 59: Whyte Museum of the Canadian Rockies, NA66 2522; Page 60: Whyte Museum of the Canadian Rockies, M282-O.S.; Page 61: Whyte Museum of the Canadian Rockies, NA33-323; Page 65: Whyte Museum of the Canadian Rockies, NA33-298; Page 66, 67: Andrew Hempstead; Page 68 (top): Edward Cavell; Page 68 (bottom): CPR Archives, repository number unknown; Page 69: Andrew Hempstead.

Chapter 5

Page 70: Whyte Museum of the Canadian Rockies (Byron Harmon), V263-NA71-3725; Page 73: Whyte Museum of the Canadian Rockies, PA 139-347; Page 74: Whyte Museum of the Canadian Rockies, NA33-797; Page 75: CPR Archives, NS.5936; Page 77: CPR Archives (Brigden's Studio), A.28394.

Chapter 6

Page 78: Whyte Museum of the Canadian Rockies (Byron Harmon), V263-NA3717; Page 81: CPR Archives, NS.1533; Page

82: CPR Archives, NS.12727; Page 85: Whyte Museum of the Canadian Rockies (Byron Harmon), V263-NA-3717; Page 86: CPR Archives (Ed Steele), NS.23847; Page 91: Fairmont Hotels & Resorts.

Chapter 7

Page 92: CPR Archives (Norman Fraser), A.6189; Page 94: Glenbow Museum (Calgary Photo Supply Co.), PA-3689-448; Page 97: CPR Archives (Nick Morant), M1947; Page 100: CPR Archives, A.6122; Page 103: CPR Archives, repository number unknown; Page 104: CPR Archives (Nick Morant), M.231; Page 107: CPR Archives, A.7292; Page 111: Glenbow Museum, NA-5660-6; Page 112: CPR Archives, M.355.

Chapter 8

Page 114: Craig Richards; Page 116: Glenbow Museum, PA-3458-14; Page 117: CPR Archives (Norman Fraser), A.6510; Page 118: Glenbow Museum *(Calgary Herald)*, NA-2864-13189-1; Page 121: photographer unknown; Page 122 (top): Craig Richards; Page 122 (bottom), 123: Andrew Hempstead; Page 124: Simon Hoyle; Page 125: Glenbow Museum (Jim Hall), NA-5654-177; Page 126: John Owen; Page 127: Simon Hoyle.

Chapter 9

Page 128, 129: Andrew Hempstead; Page 133: Rafael de Jesus; Page 134: Fairmont Hotels & Resorts; Page 135, 136: Andrew Hempstead; Page 137, 138: Fairmont Hotels & Resorts; Page 139: Andrew Hempstead.

Chapter 10

Page 140, 142: Andrew Hempstead; Page 144, 145, 146, 149: Fairmont Hotels & Resorts; Page 150: Andrew Hempstead.

Chapter 11

Page 152: Andrew Hempstead; Page 155: Canadian Golf Hall of Fame; Page 156: Glenbow Museum, NA-633-10; Page 157: CPR Archives (Nicholas Morant) M.1092; Page 158: Malcolm Tapp Collection; Page 160: Andrew Hempstead.

Appendix

Page 162, 163: Fairmont Hotels & Resorts; Page 164: Andrew Hempstead.

Every effort has been made to trace the copyright holders and we apologize for any unintentional omissions. We would be happy to insert the appropriate acknowledgements in subsequent editions.

Chapter Opener Photo Captions

Introduction
A classic Bruno Engler image of a rock climber with the Banff Springs Hotel in the background.

Chapter 1
Banff Avenue, 1887.

Chapter 2
Looking across the Bow Valley from the hotel bandstand, 1890.

Chapter 3
Banff Springs Hotel from the lower slopes of Sulphur Mountain.

Chapter 4
Workers quarrying limestone for the new hotel.

Chapter 5
Looking across at the hotel from Surprise Corner, 1920.

Chapter 6
Construction of the South Wing, 1926.

Chapter 7
A 1939 Canadian Pacific Railway brochure.

Chapter 8
Presidential Suite, 1986.

Chapter 9
The outdoor pool, with Cascade Mountain in the distance.

Chapter 10
Garden Terrace.

Chapter 11
6th hole, Banff Springs Golf Course.